# Atlantic City

# Atlantic City

by
Dirk Vanderwilt

**TOURIST TOWN** GUIDES™

Atlantic City, 3rd Edition (*Tourist Town Guides*™ series)
© 2007 by Dirk Vanderwilt

**Published by:**
Channel Lake, Inc., P.O. Box 1771, New York, NY 10156-1771
http://www.channellake.com

Author: Dirk Vanderwilt
Editors: David Pabian, Emily Wang
Cover Design: Julianna Lee
Photos (Cover and Interior): Dirk Vanderwilt

Published in October, 2007

ISBN-13: 978-0-9792043-0-2
Library of Congress Control Number: 2007902190

*Disclaimer:* The information in this book has been checked for accuracy. However, neither the publisher nor the author may be held liable for errors or omissions. *Use this book at your own risk.* To obtain the latest information, we recommend that you contact the vendors directly. If you do find an error, let us know at corrections@channellake.com.

Channel Lake, Inc. is not affiliated with the vendors mentioned in this book, and the vendors have not authorized, approved or endorsed the information contained herein. This book contains the opinions of the author, and your experience may vary.

**For more information, visit http://www.touristtown.com**

# Help Our Environment!

Even when on vacation, your responsibility to protect the environment does not end. Here are some ways you can help our planet without spoiling your fun:

✓ Ask your hotel staff not to clean your towels and bed linens each day. This reduces water waste and detergent pollution.

✓ Turn off the lights, heater, and/or air conditioner when you leave your hotel room, and keep that thermostat low!

✓ Use public transportation when available. Tourist trolleys are very popular, and they are usually cheaper and easier than a car.

✓ Recycle everything you can, and properly dispose of rubbish in labeled receptacles.

Tourist towns consume a lot of energy. Have fun, but don't be wasteful. Please do your part to ensure that these attractions are around for future generations to visit and enjoy.

**For Emily**

## COVER IMAGES

*Front cover:* the Atlantic City Boardwalk at night, the Absecon Lighthouse, and "the Show" at The Pier Shops at Caesars; *Back cover:* Atlantic City Boardwalk Hall.

**Channel Lake, Inc.**
P.O. Box 1771
New York, NY 10156

Dear Readers,

Tourist towns are a fundamental part of many vacations. Year after year, visitors arrive in droves to enjoy unique attractions. Yet these same visitors are inundated with billboards and promotional flyers that can make even a well-planned trip confusing.

This is the purpose of the *Tourist Town Guides*™ series – to keep you informed with honest, independent advice about national and regional tourist hotspots. Use these guides to look beyond all that self-serving promotion.

Many travel books fail to give tourist towns the coverage they need. *Tourist Town Guides*™ helps make sure you have the necessary information, without unnecessary clutter. Thoughtfully researched and intuitively organized, the books in this series are your comprehensive guides to all things tourist.

I am confident that you will find these guides both informative and useful, and that you will refer to them again and again. Enjoy your vacation!

Sincerely,

Dirk Vanderwilt
Executive Editor
Channel Lake, Inc.

www.touristtown.com

*Located in Atlantic City, the **Absecon Lighthouse** is the tallest lighthouse in New Jersey, and the third tallest in the United States.*

# Table of Contents

*In he earliest days of Atlantic City's existence, doctors prescribed the salty sea air as a cure for a wide variety of ailments.*

# Atlantic City Map
Boardwalk - Downbeach - Midtown

North

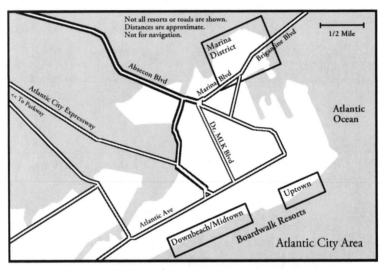

Not all resorts or roads are shown.
Distances are approximate.
Not for navigation.

1/2 Mile

Marina District

Brigantine Blvd

Absecon Blvd

Atlantic City Expressway

<< To Parkway

Marina Blvd

Dr. MLK Blvd

Atlantic Ocean

Atlantic Ave

Uptown

Downbeach/Midtown

Boardwalk Resorts

Atlantic City Area

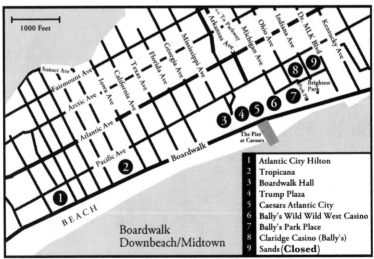

1000 Feet

Sunset Ave
Fairmount Ave
Arctic Ave
Iowa Ave
California Ave
Texas Ave
Florida Ave
Georgia Ave
Mississippi Ave
Arkansas Ave
<< To Parkway
Michigan Ave
Ohio Ave
Indiana Ave
Dr. MLK Blvd
Kentucky Ave

Atlantic Ave

Pacific Ave

Boardwalk

Brighton Park
Park Pl

The Pier at Caesars

BEACH

Boardwalk
Downbeach/Midtown

| | |
|---|---|
| 1 | Atlantic City Hilton |
| 2 | Tropicana |
| 3 | Boardwalk Hall |
| 4 | Trump Plaza |
| 5 | Caesars Atlantic City |
| 6 | Bally's Wild Wild West Casino |
| 7 | Bally's Park Place |
| 8 | Claridge Casino (Bally's) |
| 9 | Sands (**Closed**) |

# Atlantic City Map
## Uptown - Marina District

North

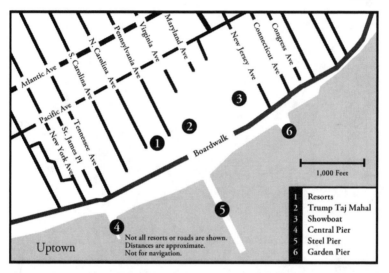

| | |
|---|---|
| 1 | Resorts |
| 2 | Trump Taj Mahal |
| 3 | Showboat |
| 4 | Central Pier |
| 5 | Steel Pier |
| 6 | Garden Pier |

1,000 Feet

Atlantic Ave
N. Carolina Ave
S. Carolina Ave
Pennsylvania Ave
Virginia Ave
Maryland Ave
New Jersey Ave
Connecticut Ave
Congress Ave
Pacific Ave
Tennessee Ave
St. James Pl
New York Ave
Boardwalk

Uptown

Not all resorts or roads are shown.
Distances are approximate.
Not for navigation.

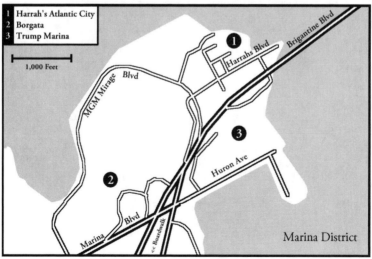

| | |
|---|---|
| 1 | Harrah's Atlantic City |
| 2 | Borgata |
| 3 | Trump Marina |

1,000 Feet

MGM Mirage Blvd
Harrahs Blvd
Brigantine Blvd
Huron Ave
Marina Blvd
<< Boardwalk

Marina District

# Introduction

*"Here beauty assembles, but it is ofttimes not the beauty of life. It is the glaring show and tinsel array of society that attracts great numbers..."*
- Orville O. Hiestand, on Atlantic City, 1922

Atlantic City is the most famous American casino gambling destination outside of Las Vegas, and with good reason. Not only is it the second most popular gambling destination in the U.S. (behind Las Vegas), but its beachfront location within the most populous region of the United States makes it a darn fine place to vacation. With about a dozen high-rise resorts and the country's first oceanside Boardwalk (with a capital "B"), it attracts thousands of people every day, and over 31 million people each year. The original version of Parker Brothers' classic game Monopoly was influenced by its street names, and the annual Miss America pageant was held here for over 80 years. Like Las Vegas, it offers visitors the possibility to win big at slots or Blackjack, stay in high quality suites, and rub elbows with the rich and famous.

Of course, however, Las Vegas it is not. Though its beachfront location is far superior to the desert oasis out west, Atlantic City's strict gambling laws and limited choices for non-gambling entertainment have given the city a more pessimistic aura since gambling was legalized (to combat decades of declining tourism) in 1976. However, even the most cynical Atlantic City critics and tourists alike have seen drastic improvements in the past several years: the luxurious Borgata resort, Atlantic City Outlets, the Quarter at Tropicana and The Pier Shops at Caesars are all contributing to this new wave of tourist improvements. In fact, the moment this book hits the press, chances are good that a new mega-attraction will surface, drawing mass media frenzy – just as the Borgata did in 2003. When that happens, this book will be a history lesson; a chapter in a halfway-completed saga of rebirth.

Atlantic City is an old city that has seen the greatest ups and the most devastating downs. Today, Atlantic City is fast, *fast* becoming the vacation destination it used to be during its glorious heyday at the turn of the 20th century. Every moment seems to bring about a new and wonderful change, drawing more tourists, making the city more diverse, and an even better place to vacation. It is still not Las Vegas, but the future looks very bright, indeed.

## HOW TO USE THIS BOOK

Items are listed within subject groups. Based on information availability, the attraction may have an address, website (✇), and/or telephone number (☎). Some items have other items within them (for example, a restaurant within a casino). In this case, the contact information may be with the inline text, or there may be no contact information. If there is no contact information, please see the attraction or section heading.

*Must-See Attractions:* Headlining must-see attractions, or those that are otherwise iconic or defining, are designated with the 🗝 symbol. The author and/or editor made these and all other qualitative value judgments.

*Coverage:* This book is not all-inclusive. It is comprehensive, with many different options for entertainment, dining, eating, shopping, etc., but there are many establishments not listed here. Since this is an independent guide, the decision of what to include was made entirely by the author and/or editor.

*Attraction Pricing:* When applicable, at the end of each attraction listing is a general pricing reference, indicated by dollar signs, relative to other attractions in the region. The scale is from "$" (least expensive) to "$$$$" (most expensive). Contact the attraction directly for specific pricing information. **Please note that** if the attraction is free, of if no pricing information is available at the time of publication, or if a price indication is otherwise irrelevant, then the dollar sign scale is omitted from the listing.

*"Family Friendly" Designations:* This book mentions attractions that may have a "family friendly" attitude. *However,* this does *not* guarantee that the attraction meets any kind of standards for you or your family. It is merely an opinion that the attraction tends to be acceptable to some families as being appropriate for children. You are urged to contact all establishments directly to avoid possibly exposing your children to something inappropriate.

*The **1964 Democratic National Convention** took place at Boardwalk Hall (the original "Convention Center").*

# Atlantic City History

If Philadelphia is independence and New York is commerce, Atlantic City is vacation! Located on Absecon Island, a thin stretch of land on the Atlantic Ocean about 10 miles long and separated from the mainland by 6 miles of uninhabited swamp, Atlantic City has been a favorite summertime destination for centuries.

## EARLY HISTORY

Long before European settlers claimed the land, it was heavily forested and served as home for the Lenni-Lenape Native Americans. Their name for the island, Absegami, means "little water," indicating the thin expanse of water separating it from the mainland. The island was largely ignored, even after New Jersey had attained statehood in 1787, because it was inaccessible from the mainland except by boat.

By 1800, Jonathon Leeds became the first permanent resident of the island. Fifty years later, only a few others had joined his descendants as residents (Leeds himself had died in the 1830s), and the community grew slowly. As these first years progressed, the name of the island was changed to Absecum, then later to Absecon.

It was Dr. Jonathon Pitney, a recent graduate of a prestigious New York college, who saw the future of Absecon Island as a major tourist destination. By 1852, he and a group of businessmen had secured the rights to build the Camden-Atlantic railroad, which would stretch from Camden, a city near Philadelphia, to Absecon Island. In a mood of corporate loyalty, Richard Osbourne, a railway engineer who helped design the basic layout, christened the railroad's destination "Atlantic City". Osbourne and Pitney together also designed the new city's streets; roads heading north-south would be named after bodies of water (Pacific, Baltic, Mediterranean, etc), and roads heading east-west would be named after states (Tennessee, South Carolina, Pennsylvania, etc).

## EARLY TOURISM

Atlantic City was incorporated in March of 1854, and that same year the first train made its way down the new line. The total trip of about 60 miles took 2.5 hours, but by the trip's end, as the first vacationers stepped off the train and onto the beach, the era of Atlantic City tourism had begun.

After 1860, Atlantic City became one of the hottest vacation destinations in America. Its primary draw – location – made it accessible from several major urban areas, particularly Philadelphia. People from all over would flock to the city's beaches to enjoy summer activities. At the time, Atlantic City focused its energies on being a health resort. Doctors would even prescribe the city's "sea air" as a remedy for stress, pain, and even insanity. As the population and tourism grew, the businesses began to expand and move closer to the beach.

There was only one problem with the close proximity to the beach – the beach itself. Merchants were inundated with sand-dragged, dropped and deposited in their establishments. In the late 1860s, railroad constructor Alex Boardman proposed a solution. Along with others, he suggested a walkway that would rise above the sand and allow beachgoers to clean their feet before leaving the beach. On June 26, 1870, the plan was realized – a wooden walkway was completed that separated the beach from the rest of the city. Boardman's Walk – as it was called – was the world's first. The name was eventually shortened to "Boardwalk". Plus, as an official Atlantic City "street", Boardwalk was (and still is) always spelled with a capital B.

As demand for additional beachfront space rose, the Boardwalk grew. This expansion led to the invention in 1884 of another Atlantic City staple, the rolling chair. A canopied chair designed to be pushed from behind, it made traveling the length of the ever-expanding Boardwalk easier for wealthy vacationers. Boardwalk real estate became a prime location. All sorts of beachside attractions sprang up, from amusement piers to sideshows to performance theaters to small vendors selling Salt Water Taffy (another Atlantic City first) and more. Steeplechase Pier, Steel Pier, Heinz Pier, the Million Dollar Pier, and others made their glorious debuts in those first few decades of rapid development.

Between 1890 and 1940, Atlantic City's history becomes less a single chain of events, but rather a series of "oddities" and "firsts." So much happened in Atlantic City during its heyday: presidents came to speak, magicians dazzled audiences, amusement piers came and went and came again, and countless other bits and pieces of history were made. Atlantic City had razzle-dazzle, craziness, in-your-face showiness, corporate enterprising, and everything in between.

The first picture postcards in the U.S. were views of Atlantic City in 1872. Salt Water Taffy was invented and named there around 1880. The first air-conditioned theater opened in the summer of 1896. Although Chicago holds fame for the first "Ferris Wheel," it was in 1891 that Williams Somers built an "observational roundabout" on the Boardwalk. It was this wheel ride that was observed and improved upon by George Washington Gale Ferris for the 1893 Chicago World's Fair, and it is his name, not Somers', that is today attached to the ride.

The string of "firsts" continued into the 20th century. In 1915, the first non-subsidized public transportation system, The Atlantic City Jitney, was established. The first passenger airline service made its way through Atlantic City in 1919, the same year that the term "airport" was coined. Of course, the Miss America pageant started here in 1921, and continued here for decades. The first official convention hall opened its doors in Atlantic City in 1929. For golfers, the slang terms "Eagle" and "Birdie" were first used here.

## THE MISS AMERICA ORGANIZATION

*(⌘ missamerica.org)* By far the most famous event to have taken place on a regular basis in Atlantic City was the annual Miss America Pageant. The first Miss America was Margaret Gorman of Washington, DC, who was crowned in 1921, and after that there was a competition every year until 1927. But when the Great Depression hit, the pageant went into hiatus for several years, while Boardwalk Hall was constructed.

The first depression-era pageant was held in 1933, the first in Boardwalk Hall. Since then, there have been a few years that lacked a Miss America, and 2003 was the 75th crowning. However, in recent years the pageant has pulled itself out of Atlantic City, and the 2006 Miss America was crowned in Las Vegas, Nevada. Though Miss America is not necessarily finished with Atlantic City, the tide is definitely turning.

Today, signs of the pageant can still be seen all over the city. Visitors will notice the street name "One Miss America Way", in addition to countless signs and Billboards touting this event. And in the weeks leading up to the finals, the city would dress up.

The Miss America Organization is officially a scholarship competition for women between the ages of 17 and 24. The organization gives out about $45 million annually in scholarship and assistance money. Though scholarships are awarded at various levels of the competition (not just in the finals), the actual title of "Miss America" is bestowed upon one woman each year. Being Miss America is actually a job unto itself – it requires extensive traveling throughout the year-long tenure, to support various organizations, charities, and other worthy causes.

Atlantic City has historically taken great pride in its hosting of Miss America. Though the pageant is gone from Atlantic City, and the main offices have since moved away, many names and places continue to pay tribute to it, as one of America's most famous institutions.

## DOWNFALL OF THE GOLDEN AGE

By 1944, the Atlantic City Boardwalk stretched a staggering seven miles down the coast of Absecon Island – ending in Longport, three cities south. However, in the fall of that year, a massive east coast hurricane destroyed most of the Boardwalk, many attractions and several amusement piers. The Boardwalk would eventually be rebuilt to a shorter distance of about 5.75 miles (including the Ventnor section).

The hurricane of 1944 may have been the straw that broke the proverbial camel's back for Atlantic City tourism. Commercial airline travel, popularized in the 1930s and 1940s, was making exotic destinations (such as Florida and the Bahamas) more accessible. There was less need for a local vacation destination, and Atlantic City tourism began its steady decline. By the 1960s, Atlantic City was dead. With almost no tourist income, high unemployment, and low population, something had to be done.

## THE NEW FACE OF ATLANTIC CITY

In 1970, a bill was introduced to the New Jersey Assembly suggesting the legalization of gambling statewide as a way to boost Atlantic City's economy. The bill was rejected and the idea dropped, partly due to pressure from protest groups against the idea of legalized gambling in New Jersey. At that point, the only state in the U.S. with legalized gambling was Nevada (established in the 1930s). Three similar gambling bills were brought to the assembly before it was finally approved in 1976, and only after the bill was modified to allow for gambling exclusively at Atlantic City, and not statewide as the previous proposals had suggested. A mere 18 months later, in May 1978, the first casino in Atlantic

City – Resorts International – opened its doors. In the ensuing years, other casinos quickly followed suit, and a new wave of tourism began.

Legalizing gambling in Atlantic City was meant to revitalize an economically and socially stagnant area. Since 1976, revenues and tourism have skyrocketed, from virtually no tourism to well over 30 million visitors each year. The money generated from gambling was intended, in part, to be invested into the community as dictated in the Casino Control Act of 1977. For years, however, little progress was made in the way of the city's revitalization. Until recently, it appeared that casino revenue went right back into the resort. Now, however, things are changing.

*With 26 years of operation, the **Sands Casino Hotel** was one of the longest-running casinos in Atlantic City. It closed November 2006.*

# Area Orientation

For many in the Northeast, summer is synonymous with the Jersey Shore. From Sandy Hook to Cape May, New Jersey has turned its Atlantic shoreline into an almost nonstop cavalcade of vacation destinations. From the quaint southern tip of Cape May to amusement-park-crammed Wildwood to the gambling hotspot of Atlantic City, the Jersey Shore is visited by millions of vacationers every year. The variety of activities is endless, with something for just about everyone.

Geographically, the Jersey Shore is a series of many beaches and long, thin islands that run down the eastern coast of the state. Much of these islands are marshland, but the section about a half-mile from the coast is packed with motels, private homes, and various beach and amusement attractions. Many of these towns have their own unique boardwalk that separates the beach from the rest of the city. These boardwalks may be lined with shops, arcades, amusement piers, casinos, or private residences. Because the Shore is largely the same throughout the 127-mile stretch, most people do not visit the entire length; they usually have one specific favorite location where they visit year after year.

In general, the Jersey Shore is densely crowded (with "bennys" – shore slang for summertime vacationers) during the summer and becomes almost a series of ghost towns in the winter. The exception to this, of course, is Atlantic City, where much of the attraction is indoors, and tourists visit year-round. If you plan on enjoying the beach, perhaps you'd better visit some other Shore destination in the summertime. But if you are looking to enjoy a resort experience with restaurants, casinos, spas, shopping, and more, then Atlantic City is for you, year-round.

# THINGS TO SEE AND DO

Atlantic City is unique in a way that separates it from most other gambling destinations – it did got get its start from gambling. In fact, people flocked to the seaside resort long, *long* before gambling was a gleam even in the eyes of Las Vegas; a city not yet founded (Las Vegas was incorporated in 1911, gambling was legalized there in 1931). They would come from miles around to stroll along the Boardwalk, lie on the beach, and enjoy summer life. So Atlantic City is not historically a gambling town; gambling is a very recent occurrence.

Atlantic City is the only area on the Jersey Shore that sees many tourists consistently year-round. The casinos – the main draw – are entirely indoors. But many of the non-casino-based activities are open year-round, so a trip to Atlantic City can be fun whenever you plan on visiting.

## CASINOS

Casino gambling, of course, is the most popular entertainment option in Atlantic City. But casinos all have a similar appearance, from here to Las Vegas and everywhere in between. They are basically huge rooms filled with slots, table games, bars, and special parlors for high-limit gamblers. Craps, blackjack, roulette, baccarat, and poker are staples of table games, and slot machines offer every imaginable way of spinning wheels to match symbols. Sure, casinos are popular and can be fun, but they don't really make Atlantic City unique.

## BEACH AND BOARDWALK

The defining characteristic of Atlantic City is its beautiful seaside location – it's what Atlantic City was named for, and the reason it exists at all! Though most people don't come to swim, access to the beach is very generous; you can walk right up to the ocean from one of many access points on the Boardwalk. You can sun-bathe or swim, but keep in mind that this beach is largely life-guard-free, so you will probably be on your own. The beach is regularly cleaned and maintained, but not as well as the other Jersey Shore destinations. However, unlike other parts of the Shore, access to Atlantic City's beach is always free!

The Atlantic City Boardwalk lines about 6 miles of beach. Most resorts populate only a 2-3 mile stretch of this famous walk. In between them are countless small souvenir shops, video ar-cades, and various food and gift stands. Many hotels also have outdoor bars that are open during nicer weather. As is to be ex-pected, a vast majority of the attractions in Atlantic City are lo-cated on the Boardwalk.

**RESORT HOTELS**

Atlantic City is home to eleven massive resort hotels, each with its own unique flair. They all have multiple dining options, enter-tainment and shopping opportunities, and most have some kind of performance venue or convention hall. Eight of the resorts are located on the Boardwalk and the remaining three are in the nearby Marina District. And of course, they all have large casi-nos.

**AMUSEMENT CENTERS**

Like California, the Jersey Shore is famous for its amusement piers - attractions stretching out onto the beach and sometimes even over the ocean. The Shore has many such piers; some large and well known, others smaller and more intimate. But they all offer much the same experience – a stroll down the Boardwalk with cotton candy and stomach-churning, thrill-inducing midway rides.

In Atlantic City today, there are a total of four amusement piers. Historically, however, there have been many more piers

that have come and gone in the early decades of the 1900s.
Heinz Pier and Steeplechase Pier have gone the way of the
winds, but The Million Dollar Pier (today The Pier Shops at
Caesars), Central Pier (on the spot of the nation's first amusement pier), and Steel Pier have stood the test of time, albeit un-
dergoing repairs and major restorations over the years.

## ENTERTAINMENT AND SPORTS
Baseball, football, hockey. Boardwalk Hall, miniature golf and
outdoor festivities. All of these are right within your grasp in Atlantic City. Freeskate in a year-round, indoor ice skating facility.
Check out a minor league Atlantic City Surf baseball game. Enjoy summertime jazz concerts or play mini-golf directly on the
Boardwalk. Check out the annual Miss America pageant and
finals at the historic Boardwalk Convention Hall. Prefer "real"
golf? The Atlantic City area has many golf courses, both public
and private, both for daily use and for members only.

## PARKS AND RECREATION
In addition to the beach and the ocean, there are other places to
relax – and get back to nature – in Atlantic City. The New Jersey
Pine Barrens are just around the corner, and the Wharton State
Forest is New Jersey's largest. Just a few miles inland, you can
enjoy a hike, canoe ride, camping trip, bike ride, picnic – just
about anything you can imagine doing in the Great Outdoors.
     For coastal bird watching and habitat exploration, the Ed-
win B. Forsythe National Wildlife Refuge is the perfect place to
visit. And it's also only a short drive up the coast from Atlantic
City. If you're more into water exploration, Gardner's Basin is a
departure point for several area day-cruises, which include fishing or sight-seeing expeditions. Lakes Bay, part of the marshy
expanse that separates island from mainland, is a windsurfer's
paradise.

## SHOPPING

The Atlantic City area is packed with shopping possibilities, both within the major resorts and outside. From retail department stores to small gift shops to outlet malls and everything in between, chances are you'll find what you're looking for in one of the area's many shopping centers. Some resorts offer plentiful shopping, some even house entire retail malls. But there is much to buy beyond the Boardwalk, with establishments ranging from quaint shopping villages to massive outlet malls.

## NIGHTLIFE

After hours, prepare for your night-owl nature to take over. All casinos are open 24 hours a day, and several of the resorts host fine dance clubs and 24-hour restaurants. Atlantic City's nightlife is both famous and infamous, so venture off the Boardwalk to find some key Jersey Shore hotspots and clubs where the party lasts all night.

# CASINO OPERATIONS

The **Casino Control Act** is largely responsible for the way Atlantic City operates today. Many of the activities and cultural attractions available to visitors exist almost exclusively because of this addendum to the New Jersey state law. The Act dictates how gambling funds are distributed and how casinos should operate. Those who enjoy Atlantic City's diverse cultural activities, entertainment, and historical monuments should be aware that gambling revenues largely influence their preservation and development. The Casino Control Act functions as follows:

The New Jersey Constitution expressly says that the state is in charge of the gambling in Atlantic City. To that effect, the Casino Control Act created the **New Jersey Casino Control**

**Commission** (Tennessee Avenue & Boardwalk, Atlantic City, 609.441.3799, www.state.nj.us/casinos/). The commission has been charged with the regulation of gambling within New Jersey, and specifically Atlantic City. The office is in charge of licenses, employment, permits, and other issues pertaining to casino gambling. Casino Control Commission offices are located in each of the casino resorts in Atlantic City on the casino floor, and readily accessible for walk-in information or complaints. The **New Jersey Department of Gaming Enforcement** (P.O. Box 047, Trenton, http://www.njdge.org), a division of the Office of Law & Public Safety, ensures that the laws and regulations set forth by the state and commission are met.

According to the Casino Control Act, in order to operate a casino within Atlantic City, the following conditions apply: (1) the casino must operate in a hotel with at least 500 rooms of 325 square feet per room or more, (2) the casino floor must be no more than 60,000 square feet. (3) For each additional 100 rooms, the casino floor may expand 10,000 square feet, up to a total of 200,000 square feet. (4) The hotel must be, in the words of the Casino Control Act, a "superior, first-class facility of exceptional quality which will help restore Atlantic City as a resort, tourist and convention destination." In addition, the commission has the authority to alter the rules of any casino game, including dictate odds, set bet sizes or change payout structure.

Atlantic City's casinos gross around forty million dollars each and every month. Much of this money goes back into the maintenance of the resorts, but a portion must be invested in the economy of New Jersey. This is the job of the **Casino Reinvestment Development Authority** (1014 Atlantic Avenue, Atlantic City, NJ, 609.347.0500). Created in 1984, the Authority is designed to utilize casino revenue to "give back" to the community by initiating various projects and to create public confidence in the value of casino gambling.

Such projects of the CRDA include partnerships with the Ocean Life Center, the Absecon Lighthouse, Sandcastle Stadium, and the Korean War Memorial. Various neighborhoods in Atlantic City and the rest of New Jersey have received help from the CRDA. It is through many of these projects and partnerships that Atlantic City has made a major comeback in recent years, in terms of both the local community and the tourism business.

The Casino Control Act also provides compulsive gamblers or any who feel they have a gambling problem the opportunity to be voluntarily placed on an exclusion list. Called the **Self-Exclusion Program**, participants may elect to place themselves on a list distributed to the casinos, which would prevent them from gambling for a specified period of time. Those on the list cannot collect winnings, receive complimentary items from casinos, or apply for casino credit.

To the credit of the Casino Control Act and its creators, Atlantic City has seen a sudden boom in commerce and a second life. The progress has been slow but steady, and each year sees an increase in tourism and activities. One day Atlantic City may be known not just for tourism and gambling, but for the local community as well. Today, the 10-mile stretch of Absecon Island is home to several communities.

In addition to Atlantic City, the island also supports the communities Margate, Ventnor, and Longport. Though these communities do not have the historical importance or commercial draw of Atlantic City, they have all at some point contributed to − or benefited from - Atlantic City's astonishing success. The main hub of commerce on the island is still the Boardwalk; over 31 million visitors make their way there every year.

# GETTING INFORMATION

The more you know about Atlantic City before you go, the more you can do, and the more fun you'll have. Not only will you better appreciate your time, the anticipation of seeing the sights will be that much greater.

## A.C. CONVENTION AND VISITORS AUTHORITY
*(☎ 888.228.4748 ⫋ atlanticcitynj.com)* For places with particularly large amounts of commerce generated by tourism, places like Atlantic City, a separate division of the Chamber of Commerce will exist. Called the "Convention & Visitor's Bureau" or "Visitor's Authority" or some other such name, this special branch of the Chamber of Commerce is dedicated to promoting tourism. If it exists, this can be the best resource for finding out about what a city has to offer tourists.

Promotional booklets and fliers containing area information (which are oftentimes full-color and beautifully designed) are funded by the businesses themselves and the Authority. Therefore, information obtained via these sources is biased, but it still offers up enough information to give visitors a thorough idea of the area's offerings.

### INDEPENDENTLY PRINTED TRAVEL GUIDES
With few exceptions, printed travel guides tend to offer a lot more information than the vacationer needs, which may result in overcomplicated vacation planning. Certain high profile destinations such as Las Vegas and Orlando have many books devoted to that specific location. Atlantic City, on the other hand, tends to be covered in books about New Jersey as a whole, or in books about the Jersey Shore. Most popular New Jersey travel guide will have information on Atlantic City.

**TRAVEL AGENTS**
Commercial travel agents make planning vacations a breeze. They can search for the best deals, book flights and hotels, make restaurant reservations, and even make special requests on your behalf. Their most important asset, however, is their personal knowledge of the destination. They can recommend places to stay and things to see and do like no book or website ever could.

However, their service comes with its own price tag, which can be avoided by simply doing your own research – travel agents have no real greater power than a well-informed customer; they just have access to the right information.

**THE INTERNET**
Travel information constantly changes, and the Internet is a great way to keep up. Unfortunately, because of the largely level playing field of web sites, it is hard to know which sites to trust and which sites to examine with a bit more skepticism.

A definitive Internet source cannot be offered here; the best advice in learning about your destination of choice would be to (1) check multiple internet sources, including promotional sites, online travel agencies, and sites with user comments, and (2) check the "official" site, if any – official, meaning the site owned by the attraction or city you are interested in.

## SEASONS

As repeat visitors soon realize, there is little to differentiate seasons in Atlantic City, other than the seasonal opening or closing of a few sporadic attractions, like outdoor amusement piers. One could successfully argue that there are only two seasons in Atlantic City – summer and any other time.

## SUMMER

*(**Average High:** 83° F, **Average Low:** 66° F)* Atlantic City was historically built for summertime fun. Today, however, the free-access beach is not nearly up to the quality of other Jersey Shore beaches, but during the hottest summer days, people gather their swimwear and head for a dip. Some of the resorts get into the beach action, too, by creating makeshift "beach bars". Summer is the most popular season, and the outdoor attractions (though few and far between) are up in full swing.

## WINTER

*(**Average High:** 45° F, **Average Low:** 25° F)* The temperature drops well below freezing, but the warm comfort of a casino resort is as big a draw as ever. Sure, the crowds dwindle a bit and bargains are more likely, but the resorts are always hopping – especially New Year's Eve, one of the most crowded days over the year.

## SPRING AND FALL

*(**Average High:** 70° F, **Average Low:** 50° F)* There is little downtime or fluctuation in crowds to the casinos, but since Atlantic City is not a true beach resort, many find no reason to visit during the hottest or coldest days, and instead opt for a spring or fall trip. Most of the outdoor attractions are

# PACKING FOR YOUR TRIP

Knowing where to go is one thing, but you'll need to pack the right equipment to have a good time. Remember, pack what you *think* you'll need. A good suitcase isn't only filled with things you know you'll use, but also what you *might* use. This section provides some tips on packing the right items for your vacation. But don't worry; if you do end up forgetting something, chances are you can buy a cheap one at your destination.

### CLOTHES AND TOILETRIES

Of course, pack to reflect your destination and your plans! Atlantic City is on the Atlantic Ocean, so wintertime is freezing and summertime can be very hot (sometimes 90 degrees Fahrenheit of more), and summertime rain and wintertime snow are common. As a guideline, it's best to pack for at least one additional day. If your trip is three nights, bring four changes of clothes. Keep in mind that many resorts in Atlantic City have laundry-cleaning capabilities; using them may reduce your overall luggage.

Basic toiletries are cheap and small and widely accessible, so even if you do forget something, in many cases they might be cheap to replace, or even free – many hotels offer free toiletry items (razors, toothbrushes, etc.) to guests upon request.

### MEDICATIONS OTHER ITEMS

Make sure you have all necessary medications with you before leaving home. Also, keep important medications close to you at all times.

Also, don't forget sunscreen, camera, film and batteries, bathing suit, sunglasses, contact lenses, warm coat, rain jacket, waist pack, purse, long socks, a nice set of clothes (for a nice dinner), packed food for munching, driver's license or photo identification (or passport if you are a non-U.S. citizen), and whatever else your vacation may call for.

## GETTING TO ATLANTIC CITY

Atlantic City's close proximity to several large population centers has been a major factor in its development as a vacation destination. Washington, D.C. is about 180 miles away. New York City is 128 miles away. Philadelphia is a mere 60 miles away. If you don't plan on driving, the Atlantic City International Airport, with services from several major airline carriers, is less than 10 miles away. Atlantic City is very friendly towards private bus charters (most resorts have a bus terminal on-property) so taking a bus is a great and inexpensive alternative to driving.

## FROM POINTS NORTH

Atlantic City is best accessed via the Garden State Parkway in New Jersey. The Parkway is easily reached from various south-bound routes, particularly I-95 if your starting point is either New York City or north. In any case, connect to the Parkway heading southbound as soon as it becomes available. This major highway winds down the east coast of the state and is the main thoroughfare for accessing all points along the Jersey Shore.

Frequent travelers of the Parkway either love it or hate it. It requires several toll stops, and sometimes it can be extremely crowded (especially during the summer months when the Jersey Shore is bustling with activity), but it is a well-maintained and attractive stretch that has a very forested look (especially to any-one leaving the congested Jersey Turnpike/I-95 area around New York City). The mile markers on the Parkway count down to 0 (ending at Cape May, the southern tip of the state), and the Atlantic City Expressway is at exit/mile 38.

## FROM POINTS EAST AND SOUTH

Traveling from Philadelphia is simply a matter of negotiating your way onto the Atlantic City Expressway and then holding tight for about 60 miles until you reach the Boardwalk. This ex-pressway is along the original route that the first railroad heading to Atlantic City was located. Atlantic City is the closest shore point to Philadelphia, which is the primary reason Atlantic City exists today. As a result, most traffic comes in and out of the city via this expressway. For Philadelphians, however, speed to the shore is traded for the more scenic route that upstate vacationers have. The tolled Atlantic City Expressway is simply a matter of getting to the shore, with little diversion along the way.

Cape May on the southern tip of New Jersey is a dead end. Without taking a seventy-plus-minute ferry or driving the long way around the Delaware Bay, you cannot access the Garden State Parkway or Atlantic City. So the best option is to find your way to the Atlantic City Expressway. This is easiest to access via I-95, which runs all the way up and down the east coast of the country (from Maine to Miami). After connecting to the Atlantic City Expressway from I-95, the drive is an additional 50 miles east to the Boardwalk.

**TAKING THE BUS**

If you live in a major urban area, such as New York City or Philadelphia, you may have the option of using one of several bus lines' casino junkets, such as those offered by **Greyhound** (800.229.9424, greyhound.com). Private bus companies offer greatly reduced fares on a round-trip casino bus ticket, and even a casino bonus (generally equitable to cash) upon arrival. Though these casino bus routes are geared towards gamblers, you do not actually have to gamble. Plus, because of the city's layout, much is accessible by walking directly from the Board-walk resorts, so you may not even need a car! Of course, a car is a necessity if you wish to explore the surrounding area (and many of the attractions in this book), or don't want to spend a good portion of your day walking up and down the two-plus mile Boardwalk resort area.

Bus service to Atlantic City casinos varies depending on de-parture city. There may be 5 buses a day or one every fifteen minutes. In New York City (from Port Authority Bus Terminal), there can be as many as 30-40 buses a day, so you can go to Atlantic City almost whenever you want. If you live in a major urban area (particularly New York City, but also Philadelphia, Washington D.C., or Baltimore, Maryland), check with your local bus service to see what kind of casino packages they offer. With the proper research and combination of low fares and casino bonuses, people can get round-trip tickets to Atlantic City for as little as $8-$10.

## BY AIR

A mere 10 miles from the Boardwalk via the Atlantic City Expressway is The **Atlantic City International Airport** (Egg Harbor Township, 609.645.7895, acairport.com, airport code: ACY). The airport services several popular commercial airlines, as well as charters, and even a heliport. Taxi and shuttle services may be available to bring you to the resort area. In addition, there are rental car agencies located within the airport, including Hertz, Avis, and Budget.

## BY TRAIN

Philadelphians have lucked out – they can use the Atlantic City Line of the **New Jersey Transit** (http://www.njtransit.com) to quickly reach the shore with minimal hassle. The Atlantic City train station is within walking distance to the Boardwalk and the midtown resort area (but there are frequent resort shuttles available if one so chooses). The station is attached to the new Atlantic City Convention Center and right across the street from the **Sheraton Hotel** (2 Miss America Way, Atlantic City, NJ, 609.344.3535) - the largest non-casino hotel in Atlantic City, which caters to conventioneers.

Though access to Atlantic City via train from New York City is possible, travelers would be forced to transfer trains at least twice (unless they use **Amtrak** (800.USA.RAIL, amtrak.com), at more than triple the price – and they would still have to transfer in Philadelphia). Plus, the trip could take in excess of five hours. In this case, a train may be fun, but it is expensive and time-consuming.

# GETTING AROUND ATLANTIC CITY

A majority of the resorts are located on a two-mile stretch of the Boardwalk, directly on the beach of the Atlantic Ocean. So walking between these resorts is a definite and common possibility. But if a long beachfront walk is not your thing, or if you want to explore beyond the Boardwalk resorts, you're going to need to secure some kind of transportation alternative to your walking shoes.

## BY CAR

If you have a car, all resorts have extensive indoor parking garages (many charge a daily use parking fee from between $2 and $4, and sometimes you can even use several resorts' garages for one daily fee).

Driving between Boardwalk resorts is accomplished via either Atlantic Avenue or Pacific Avenue, which parallels the beach. Traffic on these roads can be heavy especially during peak travel times, but since the distances between resorts are not very far, it's generally easy to reach your destination. For resorts in the Marina District, the Atlantic City Connector, accessible right off the Atlantic City Expressway is the easiest way to go back and forth between resort areas. If you are exploring non-resort areas, much of the city is on a grid. However, in the northernmost section of the City, near Gardner's Basin, some streets run diagonal, so a navigational map might be necessary.

## ATLANTIC CITY JITNEY

*(201 Pacific Avenue* ☎ *609.344.8642* ✆ *acjitney.com)* The **Atlantic City Jitney Association** was established in 1915, and today is the longest running mass transportation company that is not government-subsidized in the United States. The company operates small, 13-passenger motor coaches that make regular stops at the city's more popular tourist destinations, including all the resorts, the Absecon Lighthouse, the NJ Transit Railroad Station, Gardner's Basin, City Hall, the library, as well as the hospital and police station. The Jitney is very popular and stops very frequently 24 hours a day, seven days a week.

Jitney routes are color-coded and all routes intersect Pacific Avenue, so you should have little trouble finding the right route along this well-beaten path. Your hotel or resort host will have information about where to access the Jitney, and about routes and destinations. The Jitney fare is $1.50 per single ride (payable in cash only upon boarding), but you can purchase bulk frequent rider tickets and save a few cents.

### TRAVELING BY TAXI

Atlantic City public taxis are abundant, particularly at the major resorts and attractions. Taxi fares are expensive, but if you travel within the city limits the fare has a cap (of at least $10), so you will not have to spend more than that (most taxi fares around town will wind up being at the cap). Taxis can also be taken from the Atlantic City Airport and other areas.

### ROYAL ROLLING CHAIRS

*(114 S. New York Avenue* ☎ *609.347.7500* ✆ *rollingchairs.com)* Though Royal Rolling Chairs is a newer company (established in 2002), traveling on the Boardwalk by rolling chair is almost as old as the Boardwalk itself, and is as much a staple of the city's history as they are a fun and convenient way to get around the

Boardwalk. For a per-minute fee, up to three guests at a time can literally be pushed around on small, enclosed chairs as they are calmly brought to their Boardwalk destination. Though not much faster than walking (the chairs are, after all, pushed) they allow you to sit and enjoy the sites. The rolling chairs also operate year-round, with small plastic screens shielding the riders from the winter winds.

## TOTAL EXPRESS SHUTTLE

If you are a gambler and want to access to only the four Harrah's-operated resorts (Bally's, Caesars, Harrah's and Showboat), then Harrah's offers free shuttle service via the Total Express Shuttle. Contact a Harrah's representative for information on shuttle locations and schedules. Although the Total Express buses are nice and comfortable, the service is very limited. The Atlantic City Jitney, although less comfortable, is much more speedy, frequent, and efficient, and serves *all* resorts plus many other area attractions.

# WHERE TO STAY

When deciding to spend the night in Atlantic City, there is one critical question you must ask yourself: *will you be staying on-resort or off resort?* There are two worlds to Atlantic City commerce – on one side there are huge resort-hotels, and on the other side there is the rest of the city. There are clear disadvantages and advantages to each class of accommodation, so make sure you know what you are getting into before booking that room.

## ON-RESORT

If you are staying on-resort, chances are you'll be paying top-dollar for your room, which may cost upwards of $400 on a busy summer weekend (but can cost as low as $50 if you shop around).

You'll be in a high quality resort, large and clean, with many on-site restaurants and shops. You'll probably be in a prime location, most likely on the Boardwalk. Of course, directly within your hotel will be a large, clean, and always bustling casino. You may not need a car to get around or enjoy your vacation, since there will be much to do well within walking distance. Additionally, resort hotels offer many levels of suites. Some have fitness centers, a pool, spa, or health facility. However, these facilities may have additional cost.

**OFF-RESORT**

If you are staying off-resort, the quality, price, and location of your hotel or motel will vary significantly. You will probably not be on the Boardwalk, and you may not even be near the Boardwalk. However, your hotel/motel may offer limited shuttle service to the closest resort. You will be paying less for your room, and may have easier access to the off-Boardwalk attractions. The hotel may have a restaurant, pool, health spa, or other amenities on-site, but most do not. Also, rooms off-site do not fill up as quickly, so they may be a better option for last-minute vacations.

Since Atlantic City's busiest season is the summer, you can save a lot of money by visiting in the wintertime. You won't be able to enjoy some attractions, such as Steel Pier (Atlantic City's amusement park), but many other local attractions will be available for your entertainment. Additionally, on weekends room prices soar to about three to four times the weekday rate, and sometimes rooms are unavailable in general. During the busiest times (especially summer holidays), even the most aesthetically questionable of motels may be sold out.

*Note:* Accommodation information in this book is focused primarily on the casino resorts. In my experience, you will have more fun in Atlantic City is you stay in a casino resort. However, if you do choose to stay in a non-resort hotel, I suggest that you use an online travel agent (see "Booking a Room") for information.

## BOOKING A ROOM

There are several ways to book your hotel room. Most chain hotels (including the resorts) have their own website, and mostly you can book online from there. These sites may have special deals or packages not available elsewhere. You can also use a travel agent such as **Travelocity** (888.709.5983, travelocity.com) or **hotels.com** (800.246.8357, hotels.com). However, if you need specific accommodations, such as suites, it's recommended you call the resort or hotel directly.

# WHERE TO EAT

For many vacationers, eating is the highlight of any trip. For others, however, it is merely a short break from whatever the real attraction is. There are many, many dining possibilities in Atlantic City, often within the resorts themselves.

## FAST FOOD

The quickest, cheapest, and generally least healthy way to eat is with fast food. There are so many fast food choices along highways, in cities and towns both small and large. Some of them are drive-through, some are eat-in, but they all offer the same thing: cheap food fast.

## BUFFETS

Casino and large resorts commonly have buffet-style restaurants, where all the food is set out in a communal area, and customers are free to just walk up and take whatever they want. These are all-you-can-eat for one price places, with drinks costing extra.

## SIT-DOWN DINING

Table service at its most inexpensive and convenient casual dining choices exists in many different shapes and sizes. Appetizer, entrees, snacks and desserts are often offered. Dress is casual, though individual establishments may have their own requirements. Dining at a casual restaurant may take an hour or more.

Upscale restaurants generally have a finer ambience, more of a dress code, with better food and better service. Enjoying a fine dining restaurant can take several hours, because at these places, the ambience and service is as important as the food.

### TIPS AND TIPPING

Restaurant servers, bartenders, and the rest of the staff work largely on tips given by customers. As such, their wage is substantially lower than other occupations.

At a full service restaurant, fifteen to twenty percent (15-20%) of the total bill is a standard tip, which must be divided up between the server, bartender, and bus-person. Tipping of the host or maitre 'd is optional, depending on any special requests made (birthday cakes, special seating, etc.). Tipping at buffets is generally five to ten percent (5-10%), depending on the amount of work that is done by the server.

## LOCAL PUBLICATIONS

The best resource for Atlantic City tourism is the **Atlantic City Convention & Visitor's Authority**. With one location on the Atlantic City Expressway (mile marker 2.5) and one on the Boardwalk directly adjacent to Boardwalk Hall, The Bureau is a veritable potpourri of various pamphlets, entertainment and resort listings, and many attractions. It is a promotional service with funds provided by both the state of New Jersey and by the advertisers that use their services. Similarly, the **Atlantic City**

**Chamber of Commerce** (1125 Atlantic Avenue, Atlantic City, NJ, 609.345.4524, atlanticcitychamber.com) is closely tied with the Convention & Visitors Authority, with an emphasis on promotion as opposed to tourism.

For current, time-specific information about events, concerts, and advertisements pertinent to Atlantic City and vicinity, there are several local publications available. The largest and oldest free publication in the area is **The Atlantic City Weekly** (8025 Black Horse Pike, Suite 350, West Atlantic City, NJ, 609.646.4848, acweekly.com), which is available throughout the city at various information kiosks, including most resorts and hotels. While the paper contains some local news and current events, these stories are undermined by the plethora of advertisements pertaining to local attractions, touring shows and show times, restaurants, bars, and classifieds.

For a print publication, the daily **Press of Atlantic City** (1000 W. Washington Ave, Pleasantville, NJ, 609.272.4000, pressofatlanticcity.com) features local and national news stories, as well as classifieds, advertisements, and area information. The paper offers a subscription, or can be purchased for 50 cents at a newsstand.

The monthly magazine **Dan Klein's South Jersey Insider** (P.O. Box 829, Ocean City, NJ, 609.398.0624, shorelinker.com) also contains local entertainment and attraction information, as well as news articles focused on local interests and information. Except for special events, the information in this magazine (available for free at tourist kiosks or by paid subscription) tends to be similar month after month, as the attractions listed don't change monthly. But it is good to keep up to date with prices, operating hours, and such.

There are numerous other publications available for South Jersey and Atlantic City information. Check with your hotel reception desk upon arrival for the latest information.

# The Atlantic City Resorts

The main tourist attractions in Atlantic City are located on a two-mile stretch of the world famous **Atlantic City Boardwalk** (the first boardwalk in the country). On the southern end is the Atlantic City Hilton, and on the northern end is Harrah's Showboat. In this section, we will travel up the Boardwalk through the entire two-mile stretch and explore the area's chief tourist attractions.

The other major resort section of Atlantic City, called the **Marina District**, is home to three resort-hotels that do not have immediate beach access, and can't be gotten to by walking. Major traffic into the Marina District travels from the Boardwalk via the Atlantic City Connector, a short stretch of road, which is partially underground. It allows ultra-fast access and the ability to by-pass the rest of Atlantic City – another way to control tourist access.

All major traffic into Atlantic City comes from the west on the Atlantic City Expressway, which starts in Philadelphia and stretches all the way to the ocean, with major connectors for I-95 and the Garden State Parkway (for points upstate and in New York).

As you arrive on the Atlantic City Expressway, you'll get a great view of the backs of most of the resorts. Unlike most other types of resorts, those in Atlantic City require that you enter through their back entrance! Why is this? The fronts of the buildings face the ocean. This is true for many buildings located on beachfront property; you will not be able to see the resort for what it is until you walk out onto the Boardwalk.

Although most of the hubbub revolves around the resorts themselves, there is much to see in the sections between the hotels (small gift shops and video game arcades and even several amusement piers). These will all be noted as we walk up the Boardwalk.

## CHOOSING YOUR RESORT

If you intend to stay in one of these resort hotels, the task of deciding where to book your reservation may seem daunting. Although most resorts are located within a single two-mile line (and you can easily walk between them, sometimes without even stepping outdoors), where you stay is definitely going to be a factor in how much you enjoy yourself.

Before you cram these pages and nervously make that reservation phone call, know this – all of the resort-casinos listed in this section are fine quality, and they all have substantial similarities. You're not going to get treated like a king in one and a pauper in another. Each resort has a casino, parking facilities, various kinds of rooms, and several restaurants of various kinds. However, the resorts vary substantially on beach access, shopping and entertainment possibilities, and (of course) location.

## BOARDWALK RESORTS

America's First Boardwalk. Since the late 1800s, people have been flocking from all over the east coast to this vacation destination to bask in the sun, walk on the beach, shop or play on the Boardwalk. It is the centerpiece of Atlantic City, and perhaps of the entire Jersey Shore. It is the jewel around which the rest of Atlantic City is built. Of course, the days have changed significantly since those of yore. Casinos have largely replaced the beachside amusements and oddities that once dotted the famous two-mile stretch. But still, it is no surprise that today the Boardwalk hosts more of Atlantic City's attractions than any other part of town. If you stay and play on the Boardwalk, you are in the middle of all the action. The resorts described here have the major advantage of having direct Boardwalk and beach access. In addition, many of the resorts are interconnected in such a way that you can explore them without ever setting foot outside.

## OLD HOTELS AND NEW HOTELS

One of the most interesting and eclectic aspects of Atlantic City is the combination of old and new hotels. While many of the resorts on the Boardwalk were built since the gambling age, others are radically renovated old hotels from the late 1800s, early-mid 1900s when Atlantic City was the "Queen of Resorts". These old hotels still maintain the exterior's original charm; much the way it probably looked to the vacationers of yore. Of course, the insides are all new.

One of the original requirements for building a resort casino in Atlantic City was that the resort had to be in a newly built facility. The resorts that are in old renovated hotels (such as Claridge and Resorts) were able to by-pass this rule by making significant updates to the interiors, or by adding new wings and expanding.

It is interesting to see the eclectic nature of some of these resorts; since many have been pieced together by upgrades or acquiring and re-modeling older hotels, there is a non-conformity about more than a few of them. Crossing over from a new edition to an old edition may or may not be noticeable, depending on the quality of the patch-and-paint job and the keenness of a discerning eye.

# WHAT TO LOOK FOR

With so many resort choices both on the strip and off the strip, how does one choose where to stay? While the resorts vary on some key points, they are largely similar in the amenities they may offer.

## PRICE

Most people start to look at accommodations based on their price; which can vary significantly from resort to resort. Cheap resorts can be *really* cheap, but expensive ones can start at hundreds of dollars per night. Keep in mind, however, that you get what you pay for – don't expect five-star service at a three-star resort.

## SIZE

Atlantic City resorts are large, and generally range between about one and two thousand guest rooms divided into one or more "towers". The minimum guest room count to obtain a gambling license in New Jersey is 500, but most resorts more than double this requirement.

## CASINO

This guide makes reference in a very general way to the gambling facilities available in a given casino. It does not provide instructions or tactics on casino games. Please consult other sources for this information.

For those interested in gambling, a large casino can be impressive but very daunting. Moreover, larger casino floors don't tend to have different games, but rather more of the same games. Therefore, a 60,000 square foot casino probably has the same kinds of games as a 100,000+ square foot casino, just on a smaller scale.

Casino loyalty programs are also popular reasons to choose a particular resort. If somebody has complimentary bonuses at a particular hotel or hotel chain, they may wish to visit that casino.

## FOOD

Gambling is the main attraction in Atlantic City, and unfortunately dining options take a back seat. However, all resorts have several (sometimes more than five or six) dining choices, running the gamut from buffet or cafeteria to upscale fine cuisine. Though there are a few highlights for restaurants in Atlantic City worthy of resort-hopping, visitors can stick to the restaurants in their resort, as they will likely have a fine selection. When applicable, general restaurant price is *roughly* indicated as such: $$$ = fine dining; $$ = casual/buffet dining; $ = fast food.

*Not all restaurants have price info. Bars and lounges generally do not have a price indicator. For more specific or accurate restaurant pricing, contact the resort directly.*

## SHOPPING

While most resorts have only a basic number of shopping options, mostly gift shops and sundries, there are a few diamonds in the rough. A few resorts have elaborate shopping centers reminiscent of Las Vegas, with many upscale shops featuring clothing, jewelry, accessories, and other such merchandise.

## POOL, SPA, AND FITNESS CENTER

Unlike Las Vegas (and many other gambling destinations), Atlantic City has a beautiful stretch of Jersey Shore Beach. Because of this, the pool and fitness centers in the resorts are less important, and markedly smaller. Nonetheless, each resort has its own style of fitness center and, sometimes, a pool. Access to these facilities may not be included in accommodation price.

## SHOWS

Most resorts in Atlantic City have one large entertainment venue or showroom and several smaller venues, often within bars or clubs. Though there are occasionally resident shows in a resort, these are normally off-season, the resort showrooms are most often used by traveling performers and tours during their east coast visit.

*Atlantic City is the #4 most popular vacation destination in the United States – behind Orlando, Las Vegas, and New York. Many vacationers, however, do not stay overnight.*

# Resorts: Boardwalk Downbeach

With only two resorts, the Boardwalk Downbeach section of Atlantic City is the smallest resort area. However, these two resorts are among the best and most popular in the city, and feature upscale accommodations and lots of non-gambling entertainment. Visitors will undoubtedly make their way to the Downbeach section at some point during their visit.

## ATLANTIC CITY HILTON

*(Boston Ave & Boardwalk* ☎ *609.347.7111* ✆ *hiltonac.com)* The southernmost resort on the Boardwalk, at the very end of the resort area, is the Atlantic City Hilton. It is a classy and upscale establishment, and reliant on good old-fashioned quality and customer service rather than casino-resort tackiness to draw visitors. The Hilton is a favorite for those who enjoy a more subdued elegance rather than showiness.

The Atlantic City Hilton has changed names and ownership several times over the years. The site was originally a small motel bought by Las Vegas Golden Nugget casino mogul Steve Wynn in the early 1980s. In no time it was turned into the Atlantic City Golden Nugget and was an instant and overwhelming success. But Wynn was not happy with the strict rules of Atlantic City gambling, so he decided to sell the property to Bally's/Caesars and it was renamed Bally's Grand. When Caesars Entertainment started franchising Hilton hotels, it was renamed the Atlantic City Hilton. However, most recently, the resort was removed from Caesars (and now Harrah's) roster; it is now part of the *Resorts* collection.

## ACCOMMODATIONS

There are about 800 rooms and a selection of suites available in the Atlantic City Hilton of various sizes. Additionally, the resort received a 4-star diamond rating from AAA, which is a very rare honor to bestow upon an Atlantic City resort (most other resorts are 3-star diamond). The rooms here are somewhat larger and nicer, with more amenities than is to be expected from the other resorts.

## CASINO

The Atlantic City Hilton features a smaller casino floor, with about 60,000 feet of gaming space. It is not cramped, however, and has the latest popular slot machines and table games in an upscale and classier gaming environment. It also features **Treasure Palace**, an Asian-themed casino room, and a poker room.

## POOL AND SPA

The Atlantic City Hilton has exceptional pool and health spa facilities. The pool is indoors (open year-round), and provides an outdoor sundeck, glass walls and ceiling for added light and ambience. There is also a significant 13,000-square-foot fitness and spa center for both men and women. **Bellezza – the Salon at Hilton** features various hair care and grooming options.

## EATING AND DRINKING

The Atlantic City Hilton slightly surpasses most of the other resorts in the area when it comes to dining experiences. At the very top of the list is **Peregrines'** ($$$), which specializes in award-winning seafood dishes. For steaks, then the Atlantic City Hilton offers **The Oaks Steakhouse** ($$$).

For Italian food, **Caruso's** ($$$) offers traditional pasta entrees and a nice selection of wine. A Sunday brunch is also offered. If Asian cuisine is your preference, the **Empress Garden** ($$) serves Hunan, Szechwan, and Cantonese cuisine, and a great view of the Atlantic Ocean. Also, the **Empress Gem Noodle Bar** ($$) is located near the Treasure Palace room. The **Cornucopia Buffet** ($$) has all the fare you'd expect from an Atlantic City buffet, from shrimp and crab to chicken and ribs, with a rotating menu.

For the lightest fare or quick eats, **Horizons** ($) is open 24 hours for coffee and smaller meals, whereas **Cappuccino's** ($) offers soups and sandwiches (as well as, of course, cappuccino). Also, the **Dizzy Dolphin** bar is open year-round and overlooks the Boardwalk and beach.

## ENTERTAINMENT
The **Hilton Theater** is the main entertainment venue with the Atlantic City Hilton. With about 1,200 seats and top-class equipment, it hosts major headlining talent touring the east coast. The **Hilton Beach Bar** (when it is open) also has various free events and performers. Contact the resort for performance and ticket information.

## HILTON BEACH BAR
Capitalizing on the new wave of Atlantic City beach bars, the Hilton Beach Bar is located on the beach, accessible from the Boardwalk via a sandy ramp. Much more than a standard beach bar, however, Hilton's offers personal massages as you relax in one of their several gazebos. Also play beach volleyball or horseshoes (book in advance!) or listen to a free outdoor concert. You can even swim!

# TROPICANA CASINO & RESORT

*(Brighton Ave & Boardwalk* ☎ *609.340.4000* ✆ *tropicana.net)* In just a few short years, Tropicana went from being "just another A.C. resort" to being one of the biggest and best resorts in the city. This is mostly due to its attitude toward non-gambling entertainment. In 2004, Tropicana unveiled a Las Vegas-like shopping and entertainment complex, **The Quarter**, which was at the time unique in Atlantic City. As a whole, Tropicana is a complete destination resort. There is much shopping, dining, playing and relaxing to do without even stepping foot outside. It is indeed a comprehensive and fun place.

The Columbia Sussex Corporation, which also owns a few other casinos, currently owns the Tropicana both in Atlantic City and Las Vegas. At the beginning, however, the Ramada Corporation announced it was purchasing the Tropicana in Las Vegas, and would build a Tropicana in Atlantic City on the site of the old Ambassador Hotel. It opened in November 1981. A decade ago, Tropicana became the first hotel in Atlantic City to create a more family-friendly atmosphere that various Las Vegas resorts had attempted. The indoor Atlantic City-themed amusement park, "TropWorld", was unsuccessful, and in 1996 it was ultimately destroyed to make room for more gaming space.

### ACCOMMODATIONS
Tropicana's 2,000 guest rooms make it one of the largest hotels in Atlantic City (and larger even than the Tropicana's sister property in Las Vegas). The rooms are divided into several different towers, including the new and more expensive Havana Tower, which is closest to The Quarter complex. Tropicana offers several different levels of suites.

## CASINO

Tropicana's very large casino is spread over several sections on multiple floors. Totaling about 125,000 square feet, the casino seems smaller due to its division of gaming space, and is an attractive and lively place that caters to a wide range of tastes and budgets. Popular table games and slots are represented. The casino also features a poker room.

## POOL AND SPA

Tropicana is one of the only resorts in Atlantic City with more than one pool. The hotel boasts both an indoor and outdoor swimming pool; the indoor one is open year-round. Tropicana also has a complete health club and spa facility, including massages, a hot tub and sauna, as well as various items of fitness equipment.

## EATING AND DRINKING

Tropicana offers many choices of restaurants, bars, and lounges. For upscale dining, **Il Verdi** ($$$) is a good choice. Located immediately off the casino floor, Verdi's is one of the nicest Restaurants at Tropicana, and specializes in a wide variety of Italian choices in a sophisticated, white tablecloth-type setting. Tropicana offers other fine dining choices as well, including **Wellington's** ($$$) for steak and seafood and **Golden Dynasty** ($$$) for top-of-the-line Asian cuisine. The newer **Fiesta Buffet** ($$) features rotating food including steak, fish, and veggie, and dessert choices.

## ENTERTAINMENT

Entertainment venues at Tropicana (featuring performances of some kind) are dispersed across the complex. The main venue is the **Tropicana Showroom**, Tropicana's large-scale event center. Tickets are required for most events and are available at the box office. Smaller venues scattered around the resort are generally free and much more intimate. It is usually not important to find when and where performances will occur – just follow the noise.

### THE COMEDY STOP

With an opening in 1983, **The Comedy Stop** at Tropicana is one of the older comedy clubs in Atlantic City. There is a constantly rotating collection of both headliners and local comics. It has moved around in recent years and is now located in The Quarter. Entry to this club requires tickets purchased either at the door or in advance.

### THE MARKETPLACE

Before The Quarter, one of Tropicana's greatest features was **The MarketPlace**, a selection of shops, restaurants and entertainment. The Marketplace is basically a small shopping center and food court that is contained both within the Tropicana itself and outside, along the Boardwalk. With the exception of **Hooters**, this is a family-friendly area. There are all sorts of shops and eateries around The MarketPlace; there is even a bandstand in the central area, so you don't have to be in a casino or bar to listen to live music!

These are generally casual places with laid-back ambience and generally inexpensive fare. Among the choices are **Corky's Ribs & BBQ** ($$), which offers live music from time to time, **Adam Good Deli** ($), and **Boardwalk Favorites** ($).

For just drinks and lounging around, there are some nice choices. **Firewaters** has a huge selection of beer – 101 according to their website. It is a bar; not terribly comfortable, but if you like beer in all its manifestations, you'll be at home!

## THE QUARTER 🔲

On par with the latest in ever-expanding shopping and entertainment facilities, the newest major overhaul of the Tropicana is **The Quarter**. With a grand opening which occurred late Fall 2004, this attraction is a major step-up for any Atlantic City resort; finally resort owners are attempting once again to draw a non-gambling crowd to Atlantic City. Other resorts are doing similar things, and even some off-Boardwalk properties are catering more to the family crowd than before.

The Quarter is a shopping, dining, and entertainment facility that features a multitude of different activities for everybody. Modeled after the resorts of Old Havana, Cuba, there are shops, restaurants, shows, and more! Stepping through the gateway into this heavily-themed mall is reminiscent of the Forum Shops in Las Vegas, though on a smaller scale. The ceiling is domed, sky-painted with clouds, and the indoor "streets" and facades of the shops offer a sense of perpetual Cuban dusk.

Among the facilities: Tropicana has Atlantic City's first and only **IMAX** Theater. Additionally, there are several nightclub and lounge areas, such as **Cuba Libre** and **The Sound of Philadelphia**. **Magic Masters**, a classic in Orlando, has finally made its way to Atlantic City at Tropicana. Fine dining restaurants at The Quarter include New York's **Carmine's** ($$$), **Palm Restaurant** ($$$), **P. F. Chang's** ($$$), and **Red Square** ($$$).

Also enjoy browsing the classic American Midwest style at **The Old Farmer's Almanac General Store**. **The Spy Store** sells consumer spy equipment. Of course, there are also clothing and jewelry stores, such as **Erwin Pearl** and **Chico's** and even **Brooks Brothers**.

# Resorts: Boardwalk Midtown

The bustling and congested Midtown section of the Boardwalk is by far Atlantic City's most populous; it has the most resorts, the most guest rooms and the most casino space in one small area along the Boardwalk. It is here wherein many of most famous casino resorts are located. Its easy accessibility from the Atlantic City expressway, famous resort names and central Boardwalk location make it a very popular place.

## TRUMP PLAZA

*(Mississippi Ave & Boardwalk ☎ 609.441.6000 ✆ trumpplaza.com)*
Donald Trump's design style for his buildings has always been a kind of over-the-top gaudy flair, with everything shiny and gold-plated. As the mid-sized Trump casino, however, Trump Plaza has undergone a bit of a facelift in recent years, toning down a bit of that showy Trump "style" that has become somewhat of a design trademark. Though it is still decidedly Donald, the décor is more contemporary, the casino is a bit classier and subdued, and the rooms are generally nicer. Still, visitors familiar with Trump will definitely feel at home here. Trump Plaza has gone though several legs of history, including the "Trump World's Fair" casino, and the resort is also Donald Trump's first casino in Atlantic City.

Trump Plaza is actually a combination of one large resort casino and one much smaller casino. The smaller one was initially owned by Playboy Enterprises, but the resort did very poorly, and Trump purchased the resort and added it to his Trump Plaza complex, first as a regular resort and finally, in 1996, as a casino.

## ACCOMMODATIONS

The resort features about 900 rooms and various levels of suites. The main tower of Trump Plaza is 39-stories. The resort and the rooms have been recently renovated to reflect a more subdued, contemporary style.

## CASINO

The casino floor at Trump Plaza features about 90,000 square feet of gaming space stretched along a long, thin room, glittery with that famous Trump style. It has many favorite slot machines and table games.

## POOL AND SPA

The seventh floor of Trump Plaza houses the indoor pool and spa facilities. The pool is Olympic-style, and one of the biggest in Atlantic City. During the summer an outdoor sun deck is available. The **Plaza Spa** offers several choices for relaxation and spa treatment options, such as hot tubs, steam rooms, and saunas. Swedish and Aromatherapy massages and various body treatments are available for an extra charge. Reservations should be made in advance. Tanning beds are also available, as well as a small fitness facility with all the standard workout and cardio equipment typical of a small gym. In addition to the indoor features, there is an outside recreation facility that has two tennis courts and even shuffleboard.

## EATING AND DRINKING

As a New Yorker, Donald Trump's restaurant theme throughout the resort is New York City. The top fine Italian choice is **Roberto's Ristorante** ($$$). Located on the sixth floor of the resort, it offers standard Italian food with upscale ambience. For a more extensive wine list in a contemporary setting, there is also **EVO** ($$), with more inexpensive prices and a wide range of cocktails.

On the other hand, if steak is more your thing, check out **Max's Steakhouse** ($$$). Vegetarians beware: there is little besides steak on this carnivorous menu. This is also located on the sixth floor. Or, if you prefer Asian food, **Fortunes** ($$$) is a class act all the way with Cantonese, Mandarin, and Szechwan menu choices. For Asian food in a more casual setting, Trump Plaza is also host to **China Café** ($$), which features a well-appointed Sushi bar.

But fine dining is not the only option. **Broadway Buffet** ($$), which is located below the casino, is Trump Plaza's signature buffet. **24 Central Café** ($) is the 24-hour on-premises eatery. The **Liquid Bar** is located just inside off the Boardwalk, and is a smallish quaint place for a drink.

## SHOPPING AND ENTERTAINMENT

Trump Plaza is home to the **Plaza Showroom**, a semi-large venue (by Atlantic City standards). Tickets are required for events here, which sometimes feature various Broadway shows on tour and topical performances on occasion. If you want some free live music, be sure to catch a live musical performance at **The Beach Bar**, where you can stick around as long as you're drinking. Shopping possibilities are limited, but the resort's close proximity to Atlantic City Outlets and The Pier at Caesars make this of little concern.

## RAINFOREST CAFÉ

*( rainforestcafe.com)* A densely "wooded" themed restaurant, complete with trees, waterfalls, exotic creatures, and even a tropical rainstorm, Rainforest Café is a popular choice for families traveling with children. The food is expensive but the theme, right down to the animatronic animals, is worth it for fans of the genre. The Boardwalk entrance is temple-like. ($$)

**THE BEACH BAR**

The Beach Bar at Trump Plaza, open in the summertime, is Trump's only beach bar, and by many accounts is among the best on the Boardwalk. It is located across the Boardwalk directly on the beach. Access is via a sandy wooden walkway. The Beach Bar features live music on occasion, and is a great way to relax and drink on the beach.

## CAESARS ATLANTIC CITY

*(Arkansas Ave & Boardwalk* ☎ *609.348.4411* ✆ *caesarsac.com)* Caesars Atlantic City was the second casino to establish itself in Atlantic City, opening in 1979 as Caesars Boardwalk Regency. Although it boasts over 1,200 rooms in four different towers, the resort feels small, organized and manageable. And unlike many of the other resorts along the Boardwalk, Caesars Atlantic City has maintained its consistent branding of the property, enabling its emergence as one of the best-known and most constant landmarks on the Boardwalk. Harrah's Entertainment owns the Caesars name.

Caesars Palace, the Caesars flagship resort in Las Vegas, is still much bigger and better than this smaller Atlantic City counterpart. However, with the arrival of the much-anticipated **The Pier Shops at Caesars**, Caesars Atlantic City has become one of the premier destinations in a city that has been re-inventing itself over the past several years. It has the best location on the Boardwalk, central to much of Atlantic City's entertainment.

### ACCOMMODATIONS

Caesars Atlantic City has about 1,200 guest rooms, divided into four different towers. The oldest are the North and South Temple Towers, and the Ocean Tower. The Centurion Tower is the newest and nicest.

The **Temple Lobby** at Caesars is one of the few places in the resort reminiscent of the Roman flair in Las Vegas. On entrance to the lobby it appears that one has stepped into the cool twilight of a Roman evening. The dusky ambient lighting evokes a sense of peaceful calm, highlighting a sky-painted ceiling. Artificial torches line the second floor balconies and scattered oases of palm trees complete the scene.

## CASINO

The casino floor at Caesars Atlantic City is over 120,000 square feet – a large casino size for Atlantic City. Plus, it is particularly well-organized, bright, and easy to navigate; no complicated maze. It features all the latest slot and table games, as well as a new poker room. The second-floor casino, which is smaller, has an indoor connecting walkway to the Pier Shops.

## POOL AND SPA

Caesars has one small outdoor pool, which is only open during the summertime. Though itself the pool is unimpressive, the adjacent **Spa at Caesars** has many additional amenities, including fitness equipment, hot tubs and saunas, and various spa and massage treatments. Drink service may be available in the facility.

## EATING AND DRINKING

Caesars Atlantic City offers many dining options, from casual buffet to fine dining. On the property are several dining facilities and bars. The buffet **La Piazza** ($$) may be open for all different meals, **The Gladiator Grille** ($$) may be open for lunch, and the more upscale **Primavera** ($$) will be open for dinner. All offer basically the same quality of food, but the menu selection varies. For the most exclusive taste, head over to The **Bac-**

**chanal** ($$$) restaurant and enjoy some of the best food that Caesars Atlantic City has to offer. Additionally, **Morton's The Steakhouse** ($$$) and **Nero's Grill** ($$$) features prime cuts of steak in an upscale environment.

**Café Roma** ($$), overlooking the Boardwalk and ocean, is the only dining establishment in the hotel that is open 24 hours, and the food is not that spectacular. **Toga Bar**, located in the middle of the casino floor, is always lively and centrally accessible. On the other hand, **Forum Lounge** and **Venice Bar** are relaxing and romantic places to have a drink.

**SHOPPING**

Caesars offers several on-property shopping experiences, most of which are located past the main lobby. The casino itself is split into two floors (the non-smoking floor is significantly smaller, and located on the lobby level). Most locations in the resort converge on this central location, with escalators that will take you up to third floor dining or down to the main casino floor.

With the exception of the Pier, the shops within the hotel are generally small and limited to expensive and/or Caesars-branded. It is fun to look around for a while, but, again, don't expect this shopping experience to be like The Forum Shops at Caesars Palace.

**Caesars Exclusively** sells mostly branded merchandise. You will also find **Brandeis Jewelers**, **Oggi**, **Landau Jewelers**, and **Bellezza – the Salon at Caesars**. **Emperor's Essentials** is located just off the main lobby, as you exit the resort to the self-park garage (it is designed for last-minute impulse gifts).

**ENTERTAINMENT**

Caesars Atlantic City is also home to the **Circus Maximus Theatre**, which can seat up to 1,100 people. The venue hosts performances of all kinds – musical, comedy, even Las Vegas-style revues.

Some events are held in the smaller **Palladium Ballroom**, which can be altered to accommodate many different events. If you are in the mood for a smaller setting, Caesars has numerous smaller venues with ongoing performances nightly. Walk or ride the escalator downstairs from the Circus Maximus Theatre entrance, and you will find yourself right in the middle of **The Party Pit**. It's a section on the main casino floor with the Toga Bar, which features plasma TVs, a small dance floor, and a small stage.

Even if you don't gamble, sitting at the bar in The Party Pit can be lots of fun. Be warned, though – this area of the casino can get crowded and loud if a band is playing. Plus, if you're not here to gamble, you may not want to be around so many people who are. In any case, if it's too much commotion, nearby is an exit to the Boardwalk.

**THE PIER SHOPS AT CAESARS** 🏛️

(⌖ *thepiershopsatcaesars.com*) On the Boardwalk, directly across from Caesars Atlantic City and also accessible via an indoor walkway, The Pier Shops at Caesars is a brand new multi-level shopping and entertainment complex. With an opening during the summer of 2006, the complex continues the revolutionary recent trend of Atlantic City towards non-gambling entertainment. Built on the 500,000-square-foot pier that was formerly home to "The Shops at Ocean One", the new pier features a host of activities, including shopping, entertainment, and even a large-scale water-and-light show (located on the far end of the Pier, and called, simply, "The Show"). The same group responsible for The Forum Shops at Caesars Palace has designed this new mega-center. It is an eclectic, contemporary tourist center with four floors of activities.

"**The Show**" at the end of the pier, with regular scheduled performances, is an indoor Bellagio-style fountain show with lights and pulse-pumping music. While definitely cute and worth at least one viewing during your trip, the space limitations leave a little to be desired. It does its best and is an entertaining visual and audio delight – some of the special effects are great. The show lasts about 10 minutes, and varies depending on whether you see it during the day or at night.

The historical pier has always been an entertainment and shopping venue. Its first incarnation was as the famous Million Dollar Pier, built in 1906. For its time, the pier was massive, and almost always crowded with entertainment, from performers such as Harry Houdini to early Miss America pageants to stumping politicians to all kinds of exhibits. The Million Dollar Pier was destroyed by fire in 1912, and has undergone multiple resurrections since.

Today, it is filled with entertainment and dining choices, over 90 in total, including **Hugo Boss**, **Armani**, **Bebe**, **Phillips Seafood** and **The Continental**. The pier features great views of the ocean and the skyline, and even a houses a wedding chapel.

## BALLY'S ATLANTIC CITY

*(Park Place & Boardwalk* ☎ *609.340.2000* ✆ *ballysac.com)* If there was a perfect example of haphazard ad-hoc resort creation, Bally's Atlantic City would be pretty close to it. The resort is a collection of re-designed old hotels and a new tower. Specifically, Bally's is comprised of three separate resorts areas, which have fused together over the years. Today it is collectively one of the largest resorts in Atlantic City. Bally's Wild Wild West Casino, Bally's Park Place (the "main resort"), and Claridge Casino have combined casino floor areas to create the largest total casino

floor in Atlantic City. Two of the three areas have hotel rooms available – Bally's Park Place and the Claridge Tower - adding up to over two thousand rooms in this massive (and oftentimes confusing) complex with two different fitness/spa/pool areas. All three resort areas are located side-by-side along the Boardwalk, with Bally's Wild Wild West Casino at the southern end, Claridge Casino at the north and Bally's Park Place in between. Right next door is Caesars Atlantic City, which is owned by the same company that owns Bally's Atlantic City, Caesars Entertainment. However, Caesars and Bally's are decidedly separate, connected only by a walkway on the southern end of Bally's Wild Wild West Casino.

Bally's Park Place, the original resort of the Bally's complex, was the third resort in Atlantic City. Many years later, Park Place Entertainment (now part of Harrah's Entertainment) built The Wild Wild West Casino next door, and ultimately acquired the Claridge to the north.

The resort's total casino space, including all sections, is about 220,000 square feet, making it the largest total casino in Atlantic City and *larger than any casino in Las Vegas.* Plus, Bally's Atlantic City is located right in the middle of the Boardwalk, with easy access to many of the surrounding casinos. It is also right across from the Atlantic City Outlets, near the bus terminal and The Pier Shops at Caesars, making it an all-around ideal location. Overall, Bally's Atlantic City is an inexpensive and casual resort, always crowded, and has a perpetual "run-down" look. Of course, what it lacks in quality it makes up for in size.

## BALLY'S WILD WILD WEST CASINO

Only in a casino resort town can you go from Ancient Rome to the old American West in just a few steps. Bally's Wild Wild West is immediately adjacent to Caesars Atlantic City – which is no surprise, since the same company owns them both.

Completed in 1997, Bally's Wild Wild West Casino is perhaps the most themed casino along the strip, a fact that's very apparent from both the Boardwalk side and the street side. The exterior is designed to look like a string of old west buildings, painted with bright and pastel colors.

This casino is perhaps the only theme-based casino you will find in Atlantic City that emulates the themes of lowbrow Las Vegas hotels, though far less luxurious. Although other façades in Atlantic City exist mostly in the resort's main entrance and lobby, Bally's Wild Wild West Casino goes all out – each casino room is intricately decorated to resemble a western town during the gold rush; there is a waterfall, a general store, and many western-style buildings. It is designed to look like you are outside in the evening, strolling through a neighborhood of the Old West. There are even animatronic western folk that wish you good luck as you gamble or amble.

**ACCOMMODATIONS**
Though Bally's Wild Wild West Casino is officially a part of Bally's Park Place, the facility itself does not have any guest rooms, making it the only stand-alone casino in Atlantic City. However, guest rooms through either neighboring Bally's Park Place or Caesars are easily accessible via a series of indoor walkways.

**CASINO**
Bally's Wild Wild West Casino is a winding floor. It totals about 80,000 square feet of gaming space, and has many slot and table games in a lively western-style environment. It also has a very large race & sports book. The casino also features a large array of video poker machines, and **Coyote Kate's Slot Parlor**.

## ANIMATRONIC SHOWS

The casino features several other mini-animatronic shows scattered throughout the casino that "perform" robotic shows at regular intervals. The most elaborate of these is by the Boardwalk. Visitors entering Bally's Wild Wild West Casino from the Boardwalk's main entrance will enter a mountain scene with a sky-painted ceiling, a flowing river, and an old animatronic prospector panning for riches. The prospector welcomes visitors to the resort.

## MOUNTAIN BAR

A cool themed place to have a drink, Mountain Bar features a 90-foot bar table, live music during peak times, and a prime location in the middle of the casino. Although separated from the casino with nothing more than a series of posts, patrons really feel like you're in the Rocky Mountains, drinking suds with fellow western folk. It even features a miniature train circling above.

## EATING AND DRINKING

Dining possibilities in Bally's Wild Wild West Casino are a bit limited, and are all casual and accessible; those desiring upscale food should head over to Bally's main complex. **Gold Rush Grille** ($$) serves an array of all-American foods, including steak and seafood.

Hungry visitors mosey on over to the **Lone Star Snack Bar** ($), right next door to the Mountain Bar. This fast food establishment features sodas, hot dogs and hamburgers. Seating is very limited, but the facility is almost always open late. If you're really hungry, however, you may want to consider the **Virginia City Buffet** ($$), which has a wider selection of food than many of the other buffets in the area.

For quick sweets, donuts, soda, or other deli-style snacks are available from **Gold Tooth Gertie's Buns & Bagels** ($), which is located directly underneath the escalator connecting this casino to Caesars. It is food for fun. Sometimes they even give away free samples. And through the large kitchen windows, you can also watch the doughnuts being made as you wait in line to place your order.

## BALLY'S PARK PLACE

Bally's Park Place is the "main casino" of the Bally's complex. It is home to the large Bally's Tower where most of the resort's overnight accommodations are located, as well as **The Spa at Bally's**. Bally's Park Place was the original resort - Wild Wild West Casino was built in 1997 and the Claridge resort, though built in the 1930s, was acquired by Bally's in 2002.

Bally's Park Place was the third casino resort in Atlantic City. In the late 1970s the company bought and leveled the Marlborough-Blenheim Hotel and renovated the nearby Dennis Hotel. However, it barely surpassed the five hundred-room minimum required for a gambling license. In 1988, Bally's was the first casino to exceed one thousand rooms with the introduction of the Tower, which to this day remains one of the most noticeable buildings on the Boardwalk.

Since Bally's Park Place is Bally's main casino, and since Bally's Atlantic City is collectively the largest casino resort in Atlantic City, it is understandable that most of the buses, traffic, and pedestrian thoroughfare converge at Bally's. That, added to its ideal location—right in the middle of the Boardwalk resort area—makes Bally's Park Place one of the most popular resorts in town.

## ACCOMMODATIONS

Bally's Park Place features about 1,200 guest rooms divided in to several different sections. The older "classic" rooms are located in the former Dennis Hotel (which has been extensively renovated). The newer rooms are located within the Bally's Tower. As is to be expected, there are many different of rooms and suites to choose from, ranging from basic rooms to lavish suites

However, booking a room at Bally's Park Place means your room may be located in one of three different hotel areas: **Dennis Hotel**, **Bally's Tower**, or **Claridge Tower**. Bally's Tower is generally the most upscale, the main building is the most accessible and least expensive, and the Claridge Tower is the most recently renovated.

A note about the Claridge Tower: since Bally's added the Claridge resort to its roster of Atlantic City destinations in 2002, all Claridge rooms are now booked through the main Bally's reservation system.

## CASINO

The casino at Bally's Park Place is one huge, square box. This unimaginative shape may bode well for people looking for an easily navigable space, but it lacks the intimacy of floors with more twists and turns. The floor is about 80,000 square feet with many popular slot and table games, and a large race & sports book. The casino is inexpensive overall, with low minimum bids and plenty of low-denomination slots.

## EATING AND DRINKING

Bally's lack of fine dining within Wild Wild West is compensated with more upscale choices here. Consider **Arturo's** ($$$): an upscale dining experience with a New York style setting and Italian dining. The view here of the Boardwalk and ocean is great, and the food selection is among the best Bally's Park Place offers.

Food choices include various types of steak and fresh seafood.

**Prime Place** ($$$) is Bally's steakhouse, and one of the best in Atlantic City, earning top honors in the various restaurant review publications. Prime Place also has a self-serve salad bar as well as a great view of the Boardwalk.

For another Italian experience, try **Luna** ($$$). It is Bally's most romantic restaurant, and when weather is agreeable, you can choose to dine on their patio. They also have an extensive selection of wine – and a private dining room if you wish to hold an event.

Since Bally's Park Place is a casual and friendly resort, the selection of casual dining experiences is extensive. They have the city's only **Johnny Rockets** ($). Near the Baccarat Pit is **Noodles & Zen Sum** ($), a quick-eats Asian restaurant that attempts to emulate a sushi bar.

On the walkway connecting Park Place to the Wild Wild West Casino is a staircase that leads down to Bally's buffet: **The Sidewalk Café** ($$). This is the most removed (and most hidden) restaurant at Bally's. In addition, **Gatsby's Grill & Oyster Bar** ($$) has a very unusual selection of quick foods. They serve traditional hamburgers, chowders, fresh desserts, and have a full raw bar (clams and such). For a quick and tasty bite at any time of the day, **Animations Coffee Shop** ($$) has a lot of choice, a cute cartoon theme, and both take-out and eat-in capabilities

Want only a drink? From the upscale **Blue Martini** (with live music on occasion) to the generic but ideally-situated **Lobby Lounge**, Bally's Park Place has a limited but sufficient selection of bars and lounges.

## BIKINI BEACH BAR

In summertime, the Bikini Beach Bar is an outdoor bar and small entertainment complex located directly across from Bally's on the beach. Accessible on a wooden walkway over the sand, the bar features a wide assortment of drinks, occasional live entertainment, and a great view of the ocean.

## SHOPPING AND ENTERTAINMENT

A fundamental flaw at Bally's Park Place is their lack of any significant venues for entertainment events. There is a Main Ballroom, which can be converted to accommodate many different kinds of events, but it is small and unsuitable for anything larger than a few hundred people. Bally's is well aware of this flaw, and touts that their "big events" are hosted at the nearby Atlantic City Boardwalk Hall.

Live music is also limited. The **Blue Martini** lounge has some live performances, but that is the extent of the live entertainment options at Bally's (unless you head over to the **Mountain Bar** in the Wild Wild West Casino, which has live country music on weekends and busy times of the year). Claridge next door has a venue that seats about 550 people, which is small considering that other venues in Atlantic City can fit 2,000 people or more.

## THE SPA AT BALLY'S 🏔️

As far as Atlantic City spas are concerned, The Spa at Bally's is one of the best pool and spa facilities in Atlantic City. Until the Borgata opened, it was the undisputed king of Atlantic City resort spas. This is not to say that it is remotely comparable to the extravagant multi-acre facilities in Las Vegas, but if having a good spa facility is integral to your vacation experience, then there is really not much choice other than Bally's Park Place.

The Spa at Bally's has a very nice indoor swimming pool and several whirlpools in one central room that is nicely designed with a semi-tropical theme (with plants and few cascading fountains). There are lounge chairs surrounding the pool and private areas for massages and spa treatments. It has fitness equipment. For sporty attire and accessories, Bally's **Spa Pro Shop** is located right in the spa area. There is even the **Spa Café** within the confines of the spa area, so you can enjoy a quick and healthy bite while you relax the day away and rejuvenate. And the best part is, the facility is open year round.

## CLARIDGE

The Claridge hotel, originally built in the 1930s, was renovated for casino use and re-opened in 1981. It is the smallest casino in Atlantic City, a fact that has historically not been very good for business. In 2002 it was purchased by Bally's and renovated yet again as The Claridge Tower at Bally's. Today, The Claridge Casino Hotel is one of the few resorts in Atlantic City that has maintained its original look from the city's Heyday (other hotels have either been torn down or extensively re-modeled).

Although it is considered a "Boardwalk Resort", Claridge is not on the Boardwalk. Rather, it is one block away, overlooking Brighton Park on the Oceanside, with the view of the Atlantic Ocean further in the distance than most other Boardwalk resorts. A one-way walkway connects people form the Boardwalk to the Claridge and neighboring Sands.

### ACCOMMODATIONS

The Claridge Tower has just over 500 rooms, making it the smallest Atlantic City hotel. Claridge rooms are inquired about and booked through the main Bally's Atlantic City office. Sometimes you can choose to stay at Claridge, other times you may be forced to stay at either Bally's Tower or the Dennis Hotel, depending on how booked the hotel is for the night. In either case, if you stay at either Bally's or Claridge, you have access to all the amenities at both of them.

Claridge rooms are nice and quaint, while still maintaining a decent size. There are various levels of accommodations here as well as at Bally's main resort, but there are significantly less rooms here. Claridge is also one of the best remodeling jobs in all of Atlantic City – the resort maintains an air of the old charm, but still feels fresh and new.

## CASINO

Guest rooms and public space in the old Claridge Hotel were converted into the casino at Claridge, which is a very small and intimate space. Twisting through about 60,000 square feet on several floors, the casino features popular slot and table games. Of particular note is **PennyVille**, which has a large selection of penny and nickel slots.

## POOL AND SPA

Of particular note at Claridge is the small but nice indoor pool and fitness area. It is one of the most intimate and comfortable pool areas, which – if not too crowded – can really be relaxing. There are huge windows that let in an abundance of light (especially if it's sunny) and relaxing lounge chairs with a couple of trees scattered about. Of course, all the standard massage, spa, and fitness services are available. The fitness room is small but it has most of what is needed to get a good workout.

Though the Spa at Bally's (located at Bally's Park Place) is arguably the crown jewel of pool and spa areas in Atlantic City, the Claridge's intimate environment is a definite plus. The Spa at Bally's is the most popular but also frequently the busiest. Guests of Bally's can use both pools and spas at either Bally's or Claridge.

## BRIGHTON PARK

Separating Claridge from the Boardwalk is Brighton Park, a

pleasant and well-maintained oasis in an area otherwise inhab-
ited by parking lots and towering hotels. It is free to roam for
guests of Claridge and anybody else with a curious eye. In the
summertime, the park has a water fountain, trimmed plants
other peaceful greenery.

## PALACE THEATER AT CLARIDGE

Bally's Atlantic City suffers when it comes to live entertainment.
It does not have a major performance venue, concerts and other
events are oftentimes held at the Palace Theater at Claridge,
which still only accommodates between five and six hundred
spectators. The small size makes sense for Claridge since it is a
small resort and was once independent. For show information
and tickets, contact Bally's Atlantic City.

## EATING AND DRINKING

Claridge has a steakhouse to call its own as well, **The Twenties
Steakhouse** ($$$). It has what you'd expect: quality choices of
steak and chops, and a nice view. Of special note is the steak-
house's weekly Sunday Brunch – it gets very crowded though, so
call in advance for a reservation.

**Garden Café** ($$) takes advantage of the fact that Claridge
is not located directly on the Boardwalk – it offers a great view of
the beautiful Brighton Park and the ocean in the distance. It features a standard menu with all kinds of quick eats, from pizza to
stir-fry and sandwiches. The food is not spectacular, but the view
of the park is unique.

For quick bites, **The Bagel & Doughnut Connection** ($)
is located on the connecting platform between the two resorts.
Kind of like a local New York City bagel shop, you'll find various
cheap & filling eats, including ice cream, coffee, and cold beverages (and bagels & doughnuts, of course!).

For another last-minute choice with more substantial eats,

Claridge's quick Asian food stop is **The Fulu Noodle Bar** ($$). Located right off the main casino floor, the attraction here is the wide variety of noodle soups. Choices include stew beef, shrimp wonton, spicy chicken leg, and much more. Another choice for fast Asian food is **Wok & Roll** ($); the chain has a location within Claridge right off the casino floor. **Lucky's Bar & Lounge** occasionally features live entertainment.

# Resorts: Boardwalk Uptown

At the north end of the Atlantic City Boardwalk, just before it begins to wind around the northern tip of Absecon Island, is the most secluded resort area on the Boardwalk. In fact, a half-mile of seaside condos, empty lots, and local gift shops separate the uptown from midtown sections. However, it is here that three rather large and impressive resorts, Showboat, Trump Taj Mahal and Resorts Atlantic City can be found. Despite it being the most remote section of the Atlantic City Boardwalk, these resorts offer up some pretty spectacular entertainment and gargantuan guest room counts.

## RESORTS ATLANTIC CITY

*(1133 Boardwalk ☎ 609.344.6000 ⏍ resortsac.com)* When gambling was finally legalized in Atlantic City in 1976, the first casino to open was Resorts International, a mere 18 months later. Investors had purchased the Chalfonte-Haddon Hall hotel, and instead of building an entirely new resort, only had to do some simple renovations since the old hotel already met the 500-room minimum requirements.

The original hotel had about 1,000 rooms, but the new ownership cut the rooms down to under 600 to make room for the casino floor and other on-site amenities. On May 26th 1978, at 10:00AM, the gambling era in Atlantic City was born, as Resorts International opened its doors. Over the years, Resorts Atlantic City has had numerous owners, including Donald Trump and Merv Griffin. Today, private investors in Los Angeles own it. It is a complex that holds the unique Atlantic City title as being the first casino.

Resorts Atlantic City is the southernmost resort-hotel of the

Boardwalk's uptown area, and much of the original hotel's façade still exists. It has a classical old look, but it is easy to tell where additions have been made to the original over the years. The design today is a pleasant and colorful art deco, from the exterior to the rooms to the casino floor.

## ACCOMMODATIONS
Resorts Atlantic City has about 1,100 guest rooms in two different hotel towers. The classic tower, called the **Ocean Tower**, is part of the original hotel, which sits right on the Boardwalk. The visibly newer **Rendezvous Tower** (which opened in 2004) is 27 stories high and has standard size rooms, hot tub suites, and various other levels of rooms and suites. The Rendezvous Tower has a more contemporary exterior than the Ocean Tower.

## CASINO
The large casino floor at Resorts is about 100,000 square feet and features the latest popular slot and table games. When it opened, the Rendezvous Tower added about 24,000 feet of gaming space. The art deco motif extends throughout, and Resorts' casino has a more pleasant and laid-back atmosphere.

## POOL AND SPA
Resorts also has an indoor-outdoor pool that is open year round within its larger spa facility. The resort also has a fitness center, whirlpool, and the other expected spa amenities. They offer massages as well - Swedish, aromatherapy, and more. During summertime many these can be experienced on the outdoor deck area. Also in the summertime, there is an outdoor bar.

## EATING AND DRINKING
Dining choices at Resorts seem to go as quickly as they come, but there is always a selection of fine and casual eateries. The quin-

tessential Italian restaurant in Resorts is **Capriccio** ($$$), which overlooks the Atlantic Ocean and has a Mediterranean atmosphere. For steaks, **Gallagher's Steak House** ($$$), features a specialty New York Strip dish.

The resident buffet at Resorts, called simply, **The Buffet** ($$), touts an international cuisine, which it delivers, but don't expect too much exotic flare. For quick eats, there is **Breadsticks Café & Grill** ($), with standard quick-eats such as pizza and sandwiches.

If you're just into having a drink, **Luna Lounge** is a nice place to sit back for a few quick drinks. On occasion (particularly during the weekend evenings) there is live musical entertainment to enjoy. Also, **25 Hours** is located right on the casino floor.

## ENTERTAINMENT
In addition to the occasional live entertainment at Luna Lounge, Resorts offers two different venues, neither of which are very big. The larger **Superstar Theater** features touring celebrities and musical groups. The smaller **Screening Room** is for more intimate performances. Although the theater can accommodate smaller shows, it is ideally suited for comedy shows (which are frequently featured). Both venues (depending on the acts) require tickets to be purchased in advance.

# TRUMP TAJ MAHAL

*(1000 Boardwalk at Virginia* ☎ *609.449.1000* ✆ *trumptaj.com)* The third and newest of the three Donald Trump resorts in Atlantic City, Trump Taj Mahal is the most noticeable and largest in the uptown area. With a grand unveiling in 1990, it is also widely considered to be the best of Trump's Atlantic City resorts. In fact, until the Borgata was completed in 2003, the Trump Taj Mahal was also the newest resort in Atlantic City – a title it held

for thirteen years. It is clean, upscale, large, plush, classy, and has among the most devoted regular customers of any resort on the Boardwalk.

Due to the position and size of the building, it is also the most recognizable resort on the Boardwalk, and can be seen from miles away. As the somewhat egocentric name suggests, the Trump Taj Mahal is heavily themed with Indian royalty – and the most intricately themed of all the Trump Resorts. It encompasses over seventeen acres of almost entirely enclosed space, and it is one of the tallest buildings in New Jersey. This, coupled with one of the largest casino floors in the country, makes Trump Taj Mahal indeed a monster of a resort.

## ACCOMMODATIONS
As the tallest building in Atlantic City, towering at 51 stories high, one would expect the Trump Taj to boast the largest number of rooms. Not the case. The resort has only 1,200 rooms and suites. In addition the standard rooms, the Taj offers a variety of themed suites from which to decide. Of particular note are the large and themed hospitality suites.

## CASINO
The casino at Trump Taj Mahal, as is to be expected, is a massive winding maze of popular slot and table games. The floor is about 150,000 square feet, making it the largest single casino in Atlantic City (Bally's is larger but is actually three casinos). The casino also has a poker room and a race & sports book. The poker room is home to the ESPN **United States Poker Championships**.

## POOL AND SPA
Available to hotel guest use only, Trump Taj Mahal has an indoor pool facility that is open year-round. Additionally, there is a

full fitness, spa, and salon center that features all of the pampering one would expect. In the summertime, there is also an outdoor sundeck available.

## EATING AND DRINKING

There are about twelve restaurants and lounges in Trump Taj Mahal, ranging from casual meals and drinks to top-of-the-line quality food and service.

If you're in the mood for some fine Asian cuisine, then the best place in Trump Taj is **Dynasty** ($$$). Here they have all sorts of Asian food choices, including a nice selection of sushi and maki. Expect to pay a lot, though – this is not casual dining. Dynasty also includes **Moon**, a place to drink and meet in a secluded place during the late night, with other sushi lovers.

If you want to spend lots of money on food, you can also visit the Italian-themed **Mark Anthony's** ($$$). Here, they serve all kinds of Italian dishes, with an emphasis on brick oven pizza and tradition pasta entrees.

Lastly in the gourmet category is **Scheherazade** ($$$). This is sort of a generic high-quality restaurant with an eclectic mix of entrees, notably lobster. What really makes it special is the fact that diners can eat while overlooking Trump Taj's Baccarat pit! The Trump website claims that this restaurant is the only one in the world where visitors can watch baccarat dining.

There are several other chain restaurants in Trump Taj Mahal as well. The **Stage Deli of New York** ($$) has locations both in Atlantic City and midtown Manhattan and **Sbarro** ($) has locations all over the United States.

Since every resort-casino has to have some kind of a buffet, the Trump Taj has the **Sultan's Feast** ($$). This newly renovated restaurant has traditional buffet-style dishes. Finally, for visitors just looking for an easy-going coffee-house-style facility, the **Bombay Café** ($/$$) will grill (or steam, or wrap up) what you desire to eat, twenty-four hours a day.

Finally, if you're just looking for a drink, or a place to relax, then **The Lobby Bar** is perfect for you. This lounge also features live entertainment from time to time.

## HARD ROCK CAFÉ

*(⌁ hardrockcafe.com)* Trump Taj Mahal is also home to Atlantic City's Hard Rock Café. In the same theme restaurant vein as the Rainforest Café at Trump Plaza, here you can dine among famous pieces of rock memorabilia. The menu is about the same as other Hard Rock Cafes in the 170+ restaurant chain, but it is a lot of fun. Hard Rock Café is located directly on the Boardwalk, so if it's warm you can choose their outdoor eating area. ($$)

## SHOPPING

The shopping choices at Trump Taj are limited, though the resort does have a few knick-knack shops, selling everything from gifts to presents. Sundries are also available. Its location doesn't help much, either – it is further away from the other shopping centers, such as the Pier and the outlets, than most other Atlantic City resorts.

## ENTERTAINMENT

For a family-friendly destination, Trump Taj Mahal is a great choice – better than most other resorts in the area. In addition to them close proximity to the **Steel Pier** amusement area (see the Steel Pier section elsewhere in this book), it also has one of only a few on-resort video arcades, called **Ali Baba's Arcade**. Though the arcade is very small and not as packed with games as the casino not ten feet away, it is definitely a step in the right direction for a multi-functional resort.

Additionally, Trump Taj Mahal has two large venues to host a variety of events. **The Arena** seats a whopping 5,000 guests, and the smaller **Xanadu** Showroom can hold up to 1,400. Check with the resort's box office for more information on events and shows.

## CASBAH

*(✆ casbahclub.com)* Arguably the best (or at least the most popular) club in Atlantic City, Casbah at Trump Taj is Atlantic City's answer to New York City's Webster Hall. In this mega dance club that is hyped on billboards all across Trump Taj and the rest of Atlantic City, you can dance the night away with a huge assortment of young travelers, many of which seem to have never been to a dance club before. For those that like large and sweaty dance floors with flashing lights and pretty dancers, then Casbah is a great place to be. The drinks are expensive, and the **Casbah Café** ($$) nearby serves all kind of munchies. This is a very popular club with predominantly weekend hours and long lines. ($$).

# SHOWBOAT ATLANTIC CITY

*(801 Boardwalk* ☎ *609.343.4000 ✆ harrahs.com)* Harrah's casinos are famous for their perpetual party atmosphere, but Showboat takes this to a whole new level. As one of the livelier casinos on the Boardwalk, Showboat is billed as "The Mardi Gras Casino". It really has a more general New Orleans theme.

The Showboat first opened in 1987. Since Resorts International originally owns much of the property uptown, the land on which Showboat is built has been leased from them. Harrah's, much later (in 1998), purchased the casino.

After walking through the entrance and passing the hotel check-in area, visitors will notice that there is no place you can go other than straight. Showboat (including the casino floor) is long and thin, which makes it one of the easiest resorts to navigate. As the hotel stretches back, one long side is reserved strictly for casino activity, while the other side has some of the various restaurants and activities.

Showboat used to be one of Atlantic City's smaller resorts, but a slew of recent renovations added an entirely new hotel tower, more entertainment and gaming options, and an entirely new Boardwalk-facing façade. Today, despite its northerly location, Showboat has sprung up in popularity from a sleeper to a real gem of a resort.

## ACCOMMODATIONS

Showboat is a pleasant surprise. Showboat has two towers, the tallest being 25 stories, and 1,300 guest rooms and suites. One of the towers opened with the original hotel and the other is the result of a multi-million dollar renovation, which was completed in mid-2003. Showboat offers several different levels of room styles and well over two hundred suites. The cream of the crop for their room selection is the two Super Suites.

## CASINO

The casino floor is long and thin (as is the resort itself), and most major non-gambling activities are located on the sides of the main casino level. As such, the 120,000-square foot casino is fairly easy to navigate, and getting to and from the guest rooms is relatively easy as well. The casino features popular table and slot games and also features a simulcast race facility.

## BIG EASY SPA

Resort guests also have access to the Big Easy Spa and pool facilities. The spa features basic workout equipment and tanning booths, steam baths, hot tubs, saunas, and other amenities (including massages, by appointment). The pool is outdoors and thus is seasonal. The outdoor deck is small, with little more than a few deck chairs. **Salon International** is also available for various beautification requirements (hair, nails, and skin care).

## EATING AND DRINKING

Showboat's dining section is surprisingly diverse. Topping the list is the finer **Rib & Chophouse** ($$$), features various steaks (as the name would expect).

The newly remodeled and expanded **French Quarter Buffet** ($$) one of the better buffets in Atlantic City. It features much of the food being actually prepared right in front of the guest. The ambiance is that of a New Orleans street.

Other more casual on-site options include **Casa Di Napoli** ($$), which features Italian food, and **Royal Noodle House** ($$), which has casual Asian food on the casino floor. **Canal Street Bread and Sandwich Co.** ($) serves easy snack-type foods, such as sandwiches and pizza. Late night diners will undoubtedly visit **Mansion Café** ($$), which serves food 24-hours a day.

## SHOPPING

Showboat's shopping opportunities are unfortunately limited, especially given its remote locations. The **Ocean 11 Gift Shop** provides basic gift and sundry supplies. Many people, however, will visit Trump Taj next door, which has a bit more shopping options.

## HOUSE OF BLUES MUST SEE!

*(hob.com)* The biggest draw for Showboat of late is the unsurpassed House of Blues. For a long time, Showboat trailed the pack in terms of entertainment options. However, the opening of House of Blues in 2005, the atmosphere has completely changed. The Boardwalk portion of the resort is almost entirely devoted to this popular entertainment venue. In fact, the HOB at Showboat

is among the largest in the chain.

A complete entertainment venue of itself, the House of Blues includes a show venue, a small casino, the **House of Blues Restaurant**, and even some gift-shopping options. It is a definite plus for the otherwise barren northern end of the Boardwalk. Tickets for shows may be inquired about by contacting the resort. ($$)

*The Atlantic City Boardwalk did not get its name because it is a "walk" made of wooden "boards". Instead, it is named after Alex Boardman, a railroad worker who conceived the idea to minimize the sand being tracked into the area businesses.*

# Resorts: Marina District

Although the Atlantic City Boardwalk is by far the most famous and well-traveled section of the city, there is another area that definitely deserves attention – the Marina District. Specifically, the Marina District is a set of three resort-hotels that do not reside on the Boardwalk. The resorts in the Marina District are: Trump Marina, Harrah's Atlantic City, and the Borgata. Though not interconnected and as easily accessible as Boardwalk resorts, these are among the nicer ones in Atlantic City. This section will describe this section of the city, and the reasons why you should definitely check out these three extraordinary resorts.

Getting to the Marina District is easy from the other casinos. For visitors with cars, just follows the signs. Alternatively, take a taxi or the Atlantic City Jitney. A direct one-way trip from the Boardwalk to the Marina District by car is about five minutes.

## HARRAH'S ATLANTIC CITY

*(777 Harrah's Blvd ☎ 609.441.5600 ⌨ harrahs.com)* There are many Harrah's namesake casinos across the country. Harrah's Atlantic City was the first casino in Atlantic City to be located off the Boardwalk, in an area virtually inaccessible to pedestrians and without a beachfront. As this was a calculated risk, they compensated by making the resort a bit classier, more all encompassing, and generally nicer. Though the Borgata and other citywide renovations have dwarfed the quality of Harrah's in recent years, it still remains one of the nicest and friendliest casinos in Atlantic City.

Located on the bay side of Absecon Island (in the Marina District), Harrah's Atlantic City carries throughout the complex a nautical theme, with calming ocean wave designs and a general bluish overtone. It is a quiet resort, but a solid top-ranking contender nonetheless.

## ACCOMMODATIONS

Harrah's Atlantic City has over 1,600 guest rooms and suites in four different small towers, each 16 floors: Bayview, Atrium, Marina, and Harbour. Depending on availability, you may be able to choose your tower. The resort features several different levels of suites, as well as rooms with views of either the bay or the ocean.

## CASINO

Harrah's casino almost always seems less crowded and far less cluttered than its neighboring behemoths. The large casino floor is about 140,000 square feet and has popular slot and table games. There is also a small poker room. An aquatic, marina theme carries throughout the floor, which is easily navigable.

## POOLS AND SPA

As a compensation for the beach-free location, Harrah's Atlantic City offers two indoor pools to its guests. The **Harbour Tower Pool**, built on one of Harrah's rooftops, is suitable for families and offers basic pool amenities. It is a nice indoor pool and spa complex, which is open year-round. The pool is near the **Teen Center**, which offers video and redemption games for children.

The **Waterfront Pool** (**MUST SEE**), generally open only to adults, is one of the nicest pool areas in Atlantic City. Completely indoors (and open year-round) with a glass-domed ceiling, the pool features private cabanas, tropical trees and even a poolside bar. The pool and environment invoke feelings of a lush tropical oasis, more like Las Vegas.

Also, **Red Door Spa** is on property for your beautification and relaxation needs. The Salon caters to both men and women with massages, hairstyling, manicures, pedicures, and facials. Poolside massages (at the Waterfront Pool) are available.

## SHOPPING AND ACTIVITIES

There are only a few places to do any kind of serious shopping at Harrah's. Of course there's the standard **Harrah's Gift Shop**, with sundries and products, many stamped with Harrah's insignia. Also, **Talk of the Walk**, a chain of women's apparel in Atlantic City, has a location here.

## TEEN CENTER

Harrah's is also home to one of only a few in-resort arcade game centers for children and teenagers. **Teen Center**, near the Harbor Tower Pool, has a few arcade games and activities to keep young ones active while the grown-ups gamble. Plus, it is very small, so any potential diversion for kids will not last very long. Nonetheless, the teen center (coupled with the family-friendly Harbour Tower Pool) makes Harrah's a bit more attractive to parents vacationing with their children.

## EATING AND DRINKING

Harrah's Atlantic City has several fine dining experiences on its property. **Polistina's** ($$/$$$) is their family-style Italian restaurant. The food here is a wide selection of contemporary Italian dishes (including steak and pasta). **The Steakhouse** ($$$) is more exclusively carnivorous, with steaks, chops and others prepared in a variety of ways. Harrah's recommends that reservations be made in advance for their two fine dining eateries. Next to The Steakhouse is **Bluepoint** ($$), a raw bar with a shellfish selection, as well as some seafood and drinks.

For the more casual diner, the **Reflections Café** ($$) and **Corner Grille** ($$) serve more standard fare, such as hamburgers and pizza. **Reflections** ($/$$) is open 24 hours a day. Harrah's buffet is the **Fantasea Reef Buffet** ($$), which has great underwater decorations. Enjoy not just seafood, but a wide variety of choices for breakfast, lunch, and dinner. The most unique aspect of this buffet is, of course, the well-conceived well-executed sea theme. For drinks and a little more, **Club Cappuccino** ($) features a wide array of coffees and some light eating choices (such as sandwiches and sweets).

### EDEN LOUNGE
Whenever I visit Harrah's in the evening (be it weekday or weekend), there is always activity and fun entertainment at the Eden Lounge. It is just off the casino floor, in a large open alcove, is rarely crowded, and the musicians performing are always very talented and add much-needed energy to the whole area. This small entertainment venue has become one of my favorite places to relax in Atlantic City.

### XHIBITION BAR
In perhaps an effort to draw younger crowds to Harrah's, the circular Xhibition Bar features scantily clad bartenders, waitresses and divine drinks right in the middle of the casino floor. It's a popular and hip (if not small) lounge, and in such a central location that its almost impossible to miss.

### THE WATERFRONT
In line with the ever-expanding resort upgrades, Harrah's has unveiled the Waterfront, a dining and shopping area as part of the resort's multi-million dollar renovation. Without Atlantic City's beach at its doorstep, Harrah's has created a bit of an indoor entertainment center that includes a few mid-range retail shops, **a Waterfront Buffet** ($$), and the new Waterfront Pool. The most impressive feature of the new Waterfront is the indoor

pool, which has been designed more like a tropical oasis than a utilitarian hotel pool.

# BORGATA HOTEL CASINO & SPA 🔲

*(1 Borgata Wy* ☎ *609.317.1000* ✆ *theborgata.com)* Reinventing Atlantic City, the Borgata Hotel Casino & Spa has breathed new life into a resort destination that almost seemed hopeless. The newest casino in 13 years (it opened to the public in the summer of 2003), the Borgata is a joint venture between Boyd Gaming and the MGM Mirage Corporation, both of which own popular hotels in Las Vegas.

Atlantic City's casinos have historically catered to an older crowd; an unfortunate trait that the Borgata is determined to thwart. The Borgata shines in many ways to convince the younger, more hip, and wealthier generations to pay this seaside destination a visit. To seduce the young and hip, features include glass-blown art pieces scattered about, wide pillared archways adorning the walking paths, and some of the most comfortable furniture in the guest rooms and lounge areas.

In this respect, it has definitely done its job. In fact, the Borgata is the best overall resort in all of Atlantic City. It is the cleanest, nicest, most plush, and most expensive. It has the design of a complete destination; not just a gambling hub for seniors citizens. The spa and pool, the restaurants, the entertainment and nightlife all shine with a modern, contemporary design, a class act all the way. And without beach and Boardwalk access, visitors may almost feel like they are in Las Vegas. Almost.

## ACCOMMODATIONS
Borgata's regular guest accommodations are quite simply the best in Atlantic City. The Borgata tower, a sleek 43-story hotel, features just over 2,000 of the most comfortable, modern rooms

available. In fact, every guest feature is designed for comfort. From **The Living Room**, a resort-guest-only lounge, to the walk-in showers and extra-soft bedding in the guest rooms, Borgata seeks to surpass expectations. This luxury, however, comes at a steep price – it is the most expensive and most popular hotel in the city.

Also, Borgata offers several different levels of suites, including residences complete with dining rooms designed to seat up to twelve people.

## CASINO

Decorated in a soothing contemporary style, Borgata's classy but stuffy casino is located in one central area on the main floor of the resort. It is easy to see the size of the 125,000 square-foot area from almost any vantage point. Popular slot and table games are represented here. However, this is an expensive casino with high minimum bids, and visitors shouldn't be surprised to see a $500 slot machine. The casino also features a poker room.

## POOL AND SPA

Beach and ocean access notwithstanding, Atlantic City has never been like Vegas when it comes to pool and spa facilities, but the Borgata's **Spa and Gardens** takes the city one step closer. The resort houses an indoor pool, a full spa and fitness center. In the summertime, there is an outdoor terrace open for sunny relaxation.

The spa is located on the second floor of the hotel. The largest and most obvious section is the large indoor pool and outdoor patio. The pool area is not usually very crowded.

The Borgata also has the classic spa services, such as massage and aromatherapy, at its **Spa Toccare**. For haircuts and other salon services, the **Pierra & Carlo Salon**, and **The Barbershop** are nearby.

## SHOPPING

Borgata's shopping options mainly center around the resort's **Retail Piazza**. Here is where the majority of the Borgata's retail shops are located. It is a very pretty area, sort of reminiscent of the same company's much larger shops at Bellagio in Las Vegas. There aren't many stores hare, and the prices are beyond expensive; but it's a lot of fun to look around for a while at this classy mall-esque corner of the resort.

## EATING AND DRINKING

When it comes to food, Borgata is anything but casual. The resort is home to several high-quality restaurants and bars. The first ones you pass are **Speccio** ($$$) and **Ombra** ($$$). Both feature quality Italian food, but Ombra is also concerned with fine wine. The restaurant itself is designed to look like a huge wine cellar, with thousands of bottles of wine protected behind glass not ten feet from where you dine. The portions are small and expensive; but the wine list is very large. For steaks next door is the **Old Homestead** ($$$), which features many kinds and cuts of steak. Wolfgang Puck's restaurant, the **Wolfgang Puck American Grille** ($$), features classic American dishes in a comfortable environment.

For just drinks or a more casual food options, then the **Gypsy Bar** or the **Borgata Buffet** ($$) should be perfect. Gypsy Bar primarily serves beverages, but there is also a small assortment of food if you have the munchies for something other than buffet-style mashed potatoes and corn.

If you just want to drink, check out **B-Bar** and **Mixx**, located clear on the other side of the Ring. Both these places seem to be especially busy in the evening. Mixx actually becomes somewhat of a nightclub in the later hours.

There are several other choices of dining or drinking along

The Ring; **The Metropolitan** ($$) is open 24 hours a day and has a heavy French-type cuisine influence. Step off The Ring and into the casino and you will hit **N.O.W.** ($/$$) – cheaper Asian eats (noodles and such). **Risi Bisi** ($$) offers a relatively inexpensive Italian alternative to the formal Speccio and Ombra. The **Amphora Lounge** is a good place to eat; but you can stick around after the food is gone, since it is very much a relaxing lounge as well.

## ENTERTAINMENT

The Borgata has two major venues on its property. The smaller one is **The Music Box**, which seats about nine hundred people. Though the name suggests a musical experience, The Music Box actually hosts several different kinds of events on an ongoing basis. Of particular note is the Borgata Comedy Club, which uses The Music Box to feature local comedians (and – on occasion – a few headliners).

The larger venue in the Borgata is **The Event Center** – a very large theater which can seat over three thousand people. The Event Center handles all kinds of performances, from music to comedy and everything in between – whatever is touring at the time.

Both of these facilities are accessible right off the Borgata ring on the main floor. The Borgata Box Office has information about what shows are coming and what the ticket prices are. The Borgata Comedy Club is the only recurring show as of this writing; there is a rotation of comics.

## MIXX

Mixx is located in the far corner of the Borgata's main casino floor. It consists of two floors, two different bar areas, and several separate, private rooms. As the name suggests; it is a "mix" of personalities, both in purpose and practice. By day, it's a multinational restaurant and bar, with a very wide selection of food and drink (particularly wine, though rum and sake are also prevalent) choices. The food is a combination of Asian and Latin cuisine.

By night, Mixx becomes one mega dance club; perhaps the biggest in all of Atlantic City. Like Casbah in Taj Mahal, the Mixx nightclub has the ambiance of Webster Hall in New York City, or even Pleasure Island at Walt Disney World. It is one of the biggest non-gambling destinations at the Borgata. So for those young (or young at heart) visitors that want to break their eardrums in one of the hippest social gatherings in an Atlantic City resort, and it's a busy weekend, definitely want to check out Mixx, either by day or by night. ($/$$)

## TRUMP MARINA

*(Huron & Brigantine* ☎ *609.441.2000* ✆ *trumpmarina.com)*
Trump Marina was the second of Trump's three Atlantic City Casinos to open, and the second Marina District resort. Located directly on the water of Absecon Channel, it was initially called Trump Castle, but the name was changed after pressure from then Park Place Entertainment to prevent confusion between it and Caesars Palace in Las Vegas.

The resort carries throughout a nautical theme, with aquatic and boat-related décor. Of course, the inherent Trumpness is all there, if not a bit dated: the chandeliers, the gold-paneled everything, the shiny decorations. Above the central atrium is a large skylight that brings brightness into the resort that makes it feel very friendly and accommodating. Its clientele is decidedly younger than most Atlantic City resorts, and (particularly in the summer) there are numerous entertainment options that cater to a twenty-and-thirty something crowd.

## ACCOMMODATIONS

The resort has two towers and contains a total of about eight hundred rooms, making it the smallest resort in the Marina District of Atlantic City. The Bay Tower is the largest tower, and where most of the standard accommodations are, including a few suites. However, the Crystal Tower is exceptionally decadent, the most choices of rooms and suites.

## POOL AND SPA

Perhaps to compensate for its Marina location, the large spa facility at Trump Marina is very impressive. The entire facility spans two floors, and a surprising 120,000 square feet. It has both indoor and outdoor recreation and relaxation services. In addition to standard spa and massage services, there are outdoor tennis courts, a running track and fitness equipment. There is also an outdoor pool which, like the rest of the outdoor activities, is only open during the warmer months.

## EATING AND DRINKING

For top-of-the-line Trump dining, there is none better than **Portofino** ($$$). With great views of both the harbor and the Atlantic City skyline, Portofino offers Italian food. **Harbor View** ($$$), located directly next to the Farley Marina, also provides stunning views and specializes in a variety of seafood.

If a view of the marina or harbor is not a priority, you could try the fine **Imperial Court** ($$$), which specializes in Asian cuisine of varying sorts. Traveling from East to West, **High Steaks** ($$$) is the Trump Marina steakhouse; with a variety of quality steaks in a traditional western setting.

Casual dining choices are also available at Trump Marina. For one there's the resort's token buffet-style restaurant. The **Bayside Buffet** ($$) features standard buffet food on a rotating basis. For pizza and quick eats, **Cosimo's Pizza Café** ($) serves up a variety. The **Upstairs Café** ($$), open 24 hours a day, serves up sandwiches and other last-minute bites.

## ENTERTAINMENT

Trump Marina has four entertainment venues. The largest, **Grand Cayman**, is a ballroom that can be converted for use by many different types of entertainment events. The second main venue is **The Shell**, which is smaller but has a more traditional showroom layout. Both of these venues tend to hold headliner performances, and both will probably require tickets to be purchased in advanced to attend the events contained therein.

## THE DECK

Trump Marina draws in the younger crowds with its outdoor entertainment complex. The Deck is an outdoor bar and restaurant. Open seasonally, it is the answer to the Boardwalk resorts' on-beach bars, and features occasional live music, and lots of big, fun ambience.

## THE WAVE

The Wave is a flashy Trump nightclub – but don't expect Trump Taj Mahal's Casbah. The Wave is smaller and more intimate, with an adequate sound system. The Wave is set up to accommodate both live musicians and a D.J. Be warned, however: the club gets very crowded, particularly in the summertime. ($/$$)

## SHOPPING

Trump Marina has a small but nice selection of shops and food & drink stands. The Atlantic City women's clothing and accessories chain **Talk of the Walk** has a location here, as well as **Bernie Robbins Fine Jewelry**, with watches, jewelry, and such.

The **Mariner's Gift Shop** is Trump Marina's signature gift shop, with logo-stamped items, food, and sundries. For beauty, the on-property beauty salon is **Roberto Dino**, will all the standard beautification treatments for hair, face, nails, and whatever else that may need beautifying (reservations recommended but not required).

## THE SENATOR FRANK S. FARLEY STATE MARINA

One unique aspect of Trump Marina is the fact that it really does contain a large marina. Though Trump does not own outright the Farley State Marina, it is under their management and integrated directly with the resort. There are over 600 slips for water vessels to park. These slips can be rented in a variety of ways (for the day or for the summer, and for everything in between).

The marina is fully functional. It has electric and water services for yachts and cabin cruisers, gasoline pumps, showers, laundry, and bathroom facilities. The marina itself is owned by the New Jersey Division of Parks and Forestry, so it is not an "official" part of Trump Marina's property. It is located in a well-protected inlet with very little waves or water turbulence, the water itself is deep, and many of the Jersey Shore attractions are accessible, as the marina itself is somewhat centrally-located on the shore. **Docksider** is the Marina's official store, which sells all sorts of useful nautical thingamajigs.

*Atlantic City has been a victim of powerful hurricanes – the most recent one, in 1944, destroyed most of the Boardwalk.*

A crowded Boardwalk c. 1911

Beach Entertainers, c. 1900

Resting on the sand, c. 1900

A picturesque view from The Pier at Caesars

Christmas at the Quarter in Tropicana

Gift Shops on the Boardwalk

Brighton Park

The Jersey Shore beach, with Atlantic City in the distance

Lucy the Elephant, six stories high!

The Midtown Resort Section

Steel Pier

The Garden outside Renault Winery

The Shops of Historic Smithville

*The entire Atlantic City Boardwalk is about six miles long, but only the northernmost portion of it has casinos.*

# Amusement Centers

Roller Coasters. Midway arcades. Redemption Games. Hot dogs and cotton candy. Atlantic City's Boardwalk has a history of being jam-packed with various amusement attractions of many kinds. From roller coasters to sideshows to everything in between, Atlantic City has been host to some of the wackiest amusements on the east coast, or any coast. The Boardwalk has always been where all the action takes place – and with few exceptions, most of the amusement centers are on the same stretch they've always been.

Today the amusement centers have been toned down a bit from their illustrious past. But thrills and excitement are still around. Two of the four piers in Atlantic City are host to amusement attractions. Additionally, several smaller arcades align the Boardwalk. There are some off-property amusement attractions as well.

## STEEL PIER

*(Virginia Ave & Boardwalk* ☎ *866.386.6659* ✆ *steelpier.com)*
Steel Pier is Atlantic City's answer to the other amusement piers along the Jersey Shore. It is located directly across from the Trump Taj Mahal and is only accessible from the Boardwalk. Though not as extensive as the piers in Wildwood or Seaside Heights, Steel Pier is a definite must if you are traveling to Atlantic City with a group of youngsters.

Steel Pier first opened during Atlantic City's golden age; in 1898. Since then it has had several ups and downs like everything else in the city. When Donald Trump leased the land from Resorts to complete Trump Taj Mahal, the pier was vacant, and sometimes even used for storage. But when tourism began to rise even more, the Pier found its way to becoming an amusement center once again, focusing its attention on family entertainment.

Today, the pier has everything you'd expect. Before heading out onto it, you have your choice of many amusement park favorite foods – cotton candy, funnel cakes, corn dogs, you name it! As you enter (free admission, but pay-per-ride!) you are surrounded by midway games galore. Beyond the games are the rides – Steel Pier has the standard fare – a water flume ride, Tilt-a-Whirl, Ferris Wheel, Go-Carts, and more. No major attractions, but plenty of small ones to satisfy your amusement needs for a few hours.

Crazy Mouse is Steel Pier's claim to a roller coaster. It's the most visible from far away. However, it's not like a typical roller coaster. Think of it as a combination of those spinning teacup-style rides and a traditional track coaster – your coaster's cart spins as you make your way across the twisty track. If you tend to get a little queasy, this ride will definitely make you wish you hadn't eaten that corn dog.

Steel Pier is thin and long, making all the attractions close together – there is not much room on the pier (which also makes it feel very cramped and crowded even though there may not be many people around). By the time you make it to the eastern tip, you have seen it all. But for the real thrill-seekers (or willing sightseers) a quick helicopter ride at the end of the pier is a great experience! It will give you the opportunity to get a perfect view of the Atlantic City skyline, and to take some great aerial photographs.

### CENTRAL PIER ARCADE & SPEEDWAY

*(Tennessee Ave. & Boardwalk* ☎ *609.345.5219)* Located on the site of the world's first successful amusement pier, the Central Pier Arcade & Speedway is in the resort-devoid section of the Boardwalk between Bally's and Resorts. It is primarily a video arcade with redemption games. However, the most notable aspect of Central Pier is the large **go-cart** track way down at the

end of the pier.

But historically, Central Pier is particularly special: it is on the site of the world's first successful amusement pier: Applegate's Pier, completed in 1884. Though another amusement pier had been built just three years earlier, it was destroyed in a matter of months due to inadequate infrastructure. However, Applegate's Pier was more subdued and relaxing, offering visitors a quieter escape.

## PLAYCADE ARCADE

*(2629 Boardwalk* ☎ *playcade.com)* Between Boardwalk Hall and the Tropicana is the Playcade Arcade. As one of the largest and oldest amusement arcade centers in Atlantic City, Playcade offers diversions of various sorts. They have skill-stop slot machines, arcade and video games, redemption games, and more. The indoor facility is open year-round, sometimes until late at night.

Playcade has a wide selection of arcade games despite its smallish space. They have some new releases but mostly established classics. The redemption counter – located at the back of the establishment – has a variety of prizes for those playing redemption games.

## ATLANTIC CITY MINIATURE GOLF

*(Mississippi Ave & Boardwalk* ☎ *609.347.1661* ✆ *acminigolf.com)* With the Kennedy Plaza area is Atlantic City Miniature Golf, which occupies a very unique space. As you stroll down the Boardwalk unaware, it will undoubtedly come as an unexpected surprise. It does not fit in with the surrounding environment. But, especially if you're traveling as a family, this is one of the better diversions in Atlantic City.

Located almost immediately across from Boardwalk Hall and next to Kennedy Plaza, Atlantic City Miniature Golf looks almost temporary at first; like artificial golf greens have been laid out onto the Boardwalk and could be blown away by a stiff breeze at any time. But this is the beauty of it: instead of transporting you to a Pirate's Cove or other far-off place, it takes advantage of its very unique location. You are golfing on the Atlantic City Boardwalk.

As is to be expected, this is a very popular attraction, so expect some wait especially during the hot summer months. It is a full 18 holes of mini golf, and can take quite a chunk out of your day. But for families or couples, this can be great fun. The course is open during the evening hours as well, and twilight golfing can be especially unique.

The course is not as challenging as other mini-golf courses; this can be a disadvantage if you're a seasoned mini-golfer. But all the basics are there: waterfalls, fountains, and crazy golf greens. But what isn't basic is the beautiful beach and massive Atlantic Ocean – right next to the course. ($)

## STORYBOOK LAND
*(6415 Black Horse Pike* ☎ *609.646.0103* ✆ *storybookland.com)*
Located just outside of Atlantic City, Storybook land is a small, 20 acre theme park catering to families with young children. It is designed with classic children's stories and poems in mind, and throughout the park these stories are represented in various rides and attractions. Despite the small size, however, Storybook Land really packs a lot in.

There is a quality about Storybook Land that makes it a very attractive place to visit – it is not large and noisy like other theme parks, but rather relaxing and extremely homey. The ride selection includes: a small roller coaster, a train ride, an old-time car driving track, and several other small and gentle rides. The property is very grassy and wooded, with plenty of places to relax. Seasonally, Storybook Land has some special events. Around Halloween and Christmas, the park is dressed up for the occasions with special attractions (like a visit from Santa Claus in Christmas and a purposefully-not-scary hayride for Halloween).

Storybook Land has been owned and operated entirely independently since 1955 (it is as old as Disneyland). The yearly operating schedule is generous; they are only closed for about three months out of the year (January through March). During November and December, the park has late afternoon hours on weekends. Ticket prices are reasonable – less than $20 for the 2006 season, and included unlimited rides and attractions for the day. Repeat visitors may be interested in purchasing a season pass.

Overall, Storybook Land is a very kid-friendly amusement park without a lot of the loud, flashy entertainment options found elsewhere. ($$)

# Entertainment and Sports

In addition to the venues within the main resort hotels, Atlantic City boasts several prime locations for shows, entertainment, and sporting events. Some of the places listed here (such as Boardwalk Hall) have historical significance as well as current implementations. Unlike Las Vegas, much of Atlantic City's entertainment and sport venues are integrated with the local community, New Jersey as a whole, and Philadelphia. They are treated not as stand-alone theaters designed for one resident act, but rather as a venue for touring celebrities and groups.

## BOARDWALK HALL 🅼🅸

*(2301 Boardwalk ☎ 609.348.7000 ✍ boardwalkhall.com)* The Atlantic City Boardwalk Hall was first conceived of in 1910, and eventually manifested into a building for its grand opening on May 31, 1929. Back then it was called the Atlantic City Convention Hall, but since the opening of the newer off-Boardwalk convention center in 1997, the original is now referred to as the "Boardwalk Hall". It is located near the southern section of the Boardwalk, in between the midtown and downbeach resort areas. Directly on the other side of the convention center is Kennedy Plaza, which hosts seasonal activities such as concerts and mini-golf.

Declared a National Historic Landmark in 1987, the building underwent extensive renovations and restorations, including making better use of the space for various technological innovations that were not available during the building's initial opening. There was an additional renovation in 2001, costing about $90 million, which finally brought the Hall up to par with the best venues around the country.

The building's exterior has a semi-circle shape, with a hard concrete texture. It has that "historic" look which is much different than the surrounding resort-hotels. It has a subdued, classically elegant appeal and lays much lower than the neighboring towers. While entering from the street side is less-than-attractive (you will see various utilitarian entrances and garbage pick-up stations), the Boardwalk entrance is grand, and a real step back into the history of Atlantic City architecture.

The Atlantic City Boardwalk Hall has two different venues, which can host a variety of different kinds of events. The main Hall is used for boxing, hockey and other sports, as well as concert events or shows. It is the largest single event center in Atlantic City, which can accommodate over thirteen thousand people. The Hall has hosted Boardwalk Bullies Hockey Club, Card-Sharks Indoor Football, and the Miss America Pageant. On occasion, neighboring casinos such as Bally's will take advantage of the Adrian Phillips Ballroom, since Bally's does not have a large venue of its own. The well-known SMG management company, headquartered in Philadelphia, manages the entire venue.

Boardwalk Hall can be host to several different kinds of sporting events. Atlantic City's East Coast Hockey League (ECHL) team, The Boardwalk Bullies, considers the hall its home arena. The season runs standard for minor league hockey, starting around late October. Also, brand new in the spring of 2004, is the inaugural season of New Jersey's only professional indoor football team, the Atlantic City CardSharks.

In addition, the Ultimate Fighting Championship holds occasional events here, as well as professional boxing matches, and countless concert tours. As it is the largest venue in Atlantic City, many big names are drawn to the hall. If you are interested in visiting or would like to know about a specific event, you can inquire by contacting Boardwalk Hall's box office, or online at Ticketmaster.

## ATLANTIC CITY AIR SHOW 🏷️

*(Atlantic City Boardwalk ℰ atlanticcityairshow.com)* One of the most popular seasonal events in Atlantic City is the annual Atlantic City Air Show. The sky over the Atlantic Ocean becomes a stage for wild aerial antics, stunts, military planes, and a wide range of sky-centric performances. Down below, on the Boardwalk, over a quarter million people gather to watch the event annually. This is an extremely popular free (!) event that draws more people to the Atlantic City Boardwalk than any other time of year. It is a real crowd pleaser and lots of fun for the whole family. For specific date information, visit their website.

## KENNEDY PLAZA

*(Georgia Avenue & Boardwalk)* Directly across from the Atlantic City Boardwalk Hall is Kennedy Plaza, which is, among other things, a restful showcase and stage, and an outdoor garden. The plaza fits in well with its Boardwalk Hall counterpart on the opposite side of the Boardwalk. It is partitioned from the beach with a large stone structure, complete with evenly spaced pedestals. As with the Hall itself, it feels very structurally permanent, with well-groomed and maintained stone décor. Although accessible and open free to the public year-round, it is particularly stunning during the summertime, when the flowers and plants within the garden are at their peak of color.

In the center of the plaza is a statue of a worker. The large stone plaque next to it is dedicated to people that passed away while working on Atlantic City's redevelopment since 1979. The statue was erected on April 28, 1998 and serves as a centerpiece for the plaza. Beyond the statue, against the far back of Kennedy Plaza, is a bust of John F. Kennedy himself.

Of particular note to perform on stage at Kennedy Plaza is the Chicken Bone Beach Jazz Concert Series. Every summer on a weekly schedule, groups sponsored by the Chicken Bone Beach society perform at the plaza to commemorate African-American heritage in Atlantic City. Chicken Bone Beach – the unofficially dubbed strip of beachfront south of Missouri Avenue – was where African-American families wishing to vacation in Atlantic City were restricted between the 1900s and the 1950s.

## SKATE ZONE

*(501 N. Albany Avenue* ☎ *609.441.1780* ✆ *flyerssskatezone.com)* The Philadelphia Flyers Skate Zone is a chain of family-friendly indoor ice skating facilities owned by Comcast-Spectacor (parent company of the Philadelphia Flyers as well as other sport teams and venues). Headquartered in Philadelphia, they operate area facilities in several locations, including Voorhees, Bethlehem, Pennsauken, and Atlantic City.

The Atlantic City facility opened in 1999, and caters to local interests. Several clubs and local groups make use of the indoor rink, which is open nearly year-round. Groups that use the facility include: Atlantic City Jr. Bullies Hockey Club, Atlantic City Figure Skating Club, Flyer's Youth Hockey League, Old Men's Hockey League, and several others. There is also almost always daily rink time (call for schedule) devoted to free skating, and is open to the public.

The facility is equipped to rent skates, as well as a pro shop ("Pro Zone"), a small arcade, a snack bar ("Snack Zone"), and, of course an ice rink with an audience capacity of about 300. ($$)

## SANDCASTLE BASEBALL STADIUM

*(545 North Albany Avenue* ☎ *609.344.SURF* ✆ *acsurf.com)* The Atlantic City Surf, a team in the minor league Atlantic League of Professional Baseball (ALPB). Their home ballpark is Sandcastle Baseball stadium, right next to Flyers Skate Zone on Albany Avenue.

Sandcastle Stadium is angled perfectly for a great view of

Atlantic City while in the bleachers: the baseball diamond in the foreground, and the Atlantic City skyline way in the distance. The stadium seats 5,900 spectators at capacity. Public admission to the facility is limited to sporting events; tours are generally not available.

Admission tickets for home games of the Atlantic City Surf can be purchased at The Sandcastle, or through the team's website. Seating choices include a variety of levels, from standard seats to deluxe and premium box seats. ($/$$)

# GOLF COURSES

Golfing is a big deal on the Jersey Shore, and the area is peppered with golf courses with different sizes and abilities. Although no professional courses are directly within Atlantic City, a short drive inland can be fruitful for anybody wishing to enjoy a day on one of the area's courses. Pay-per-day rates for these facilities can cost around $60-$100, depending on when in the week, or what time of day you wish to golf. Following is a select list of public golf courses.

### BLUE HERON PINES GOLF CLUB
*(550 West Country Club Drive,* ✆ *blueheronpines.com)* Blue Heron Pines Golf Club is a pay-per-game facility that offers two different 18-hole courses to choose from. Frequent golfers can also enjoy various levels of membership that allow course access on a more regular basis. On occasion, golf packages may be available with select area resorts and hotels.

### TWISTED DUNE GOLF CLUB
*(2101 Ocean Height Avenue, Egg Harbor Township, NJ,* ☎ *609.653.8019,* ✆ *twisteddune.com)* The Empire Golf Management is responsible for the daily management of several

courses around the greater Atlantic City area. One of their public courses in particular, the Twisted Dune Golf Club offers 18 holes of various ratings, as well as practice and teaching facilities.

## HARBOR PINES GOLF CLUB

*(500 St. Andrews Dr,* ☎ *609.927.0006,* ✆ *harborpines.com)* **Harbor Pines Golf Club** is a pay-per-day 18-hole golf course, which also features a collection of on-site homes in gated community style, called "Harbor Pine Estates". The course's clubhouse is particularly large and well-appointed. Of course, membership options are also available for frequent golf enthusiasts.

## SEAVIEW RESORT AND SPA

*(401 South New York Road, Galloway Township, NJ* ✆ *seaviewgolf.com)* For a more all-encompassing golf outing, Seaview Resort and Spa by Marriott is a complete resort complex that has all kinds of activities, as well as two full 18-hole golf courses. Though it particularly caters to golfers, the resort has tennis courts, indoor and outdoor pools, business meeting space, an on-site restaurant, and a full health club.

## ATLANTIC CITY COUNTRY CLUB

*(*✆ *harborpines.com)* If you wish to experience a private country club but without all the fees involved, the Atlantic City Country Club is open only to those guests staying in an area resort owned by Harrah's Entertainment For more information about this golf experience, contact the Harrah's Entertainment resort you wish to stay at prior to booking.

*Absecon Island, on which Atlantic City sits, is about six miles off the coast of New Jersey.*

# Museums and Culture

In 2004, Atlantic City celebrated its 150th anniversary. Though the attractions and culture have changed dramatically since 1854, it is a history still alive today in many of the area's attractions, the city's structure and commerce. Visitors will appreciate today's attractions and development all the more with an understanding of the city's past. Over time, many important historical figures have graced the beaches and Boardwalk, each leaving their mark. Many firsts, many oddities, and many corporate trials found their way to this spot on the coast. Visitors are often amazed to learn that there is much more to Atlantic City's value than beach resort casinos. As a testament to its long and winding history, the Atlantic City of today is host to many cultural options, from museums to monuments and memorials. Some attractions are preserved relics from the past, while others are newer additions to a constantly expanding city. The attractions listed here are located both on and off the Boardwalk.

## GARDEN PIER

*(New Jersey Ave & Boardwalk)* Historically, Garden Pier has always been the calmest pier in Atlantic City. When it first opened to the public in 1913, it was an outdoor theater, decorated with ornate flowers and plants. If you were looking for an afternoon of cultural refinement and sun, your only option in Atlantic City was the Garden Pier.

This is also true today. As the northernmost pier, it is located immediately across from the largely undeveloped lot just north of Showboat. The surrounding area is barren and uninviting, but the Garden Pier is a definite cultural highlight of the city. It is host to two distinct buildings. The Art Center is to the left as you enter the Pier's steel gate, and the Historical Museum is on the right.

## ATLANTIC CITY HISTORICAL MUSEUM

*(Garden Pier,* ☎ *609.347.5839,* ✆ *acmuseum.org)* The Atlantic City Historical Museum features comprehensive displays highlighting important moments in Atlantic City history. The museum is a small room, but in fact jam-packed with articles and information. The museum is a great start to Atlantic City's first 100 years. It features a permanent exhibit, called "Atlantic City, Playground of the Nation" with all kinds of memorabilia such as souvenirs, photos, clothes, and posters. Visitors can learn about the Boardwalk, the many amusement piers that have come and gone, and the political and corporate giants (such as H.J Heinz and George Tilyou) that have graced the city. Of particular note is the wide array of Miss America-related articles.

The museum also showcases a documentary on Atlantic City history, called "Boardwalk Ballyhoo: The Magic of Atlantic City". Copies of the documentary can be purchased at the small gift stand at the entrance to the museum. The stand also sells some very informative historical books, and some unique gift items. On occasion, the museum houses temporary exhibits. ($)

## ATLANTIC CITY ART CENTER

*(*☎ *609.347.5837)* Also located on garden pier, next door to the museum, is the Atlantic City Art Center. Though not focused on historical interests like its next-door neighbor, it houses three galleries featuring a rotating schedule of art exhibits. Overall, the Atlantic City Cultural Center on Garden Pier is a definite must-see for any first time visitor to Atlantic City. ($)

## THE NEW JERSEY KOREAN WAR MEMORIAL

*(Brighton Park & Boardwalk)* Almost exactly where Park Place meets the Boardwalk, sandwiched between Brighton Park and Bally's Park Place, is the New Jersey Korean War Memorial. It is

accessible immediately off the Boardwalk. As you enter the small enclave, you first notice two distinct walls, one made of granite and etched with names of servicemen who died during the Korean War, and one of sand-colored stone, with reliefs of American soldiers charging out of it. A statue in the center is of a single soldier, with his helmet off, holding onto several ID tags. In warmer weather, water cascades down from the memorial wall.

This is a totally free outdoor memorial dedicated to those who fought in the Korean War. Around 250 people attended the groundbreaking on March 14, 2000, and it opened to the public on November 13 that same year. It is a touching tribute to those who served; those who returned, and those who did not.

## DANTE HALL THEATER OF THE ARTS
*(14 N. Mississippi Ave* ☎ *609.344.8877* ✆ *dantehall.org)* Not a stone's throw from the gaudy (lovingly so, of course) entertainment of the casinos on boardwalk is Atlantic City's answer to classic culture. Dante Hall is – as the name suggests – a fine performing arts venue that has a regular calendar of predominately musical productions (check the website for schedules). The theater was built in 1926 and had fallen into great disrepair. Now completely renovated (in 2003), performances at Dante Hall are once again regular.

## CIVIL RIGHTS GARDEN
The Civil Rights Garden is a small garden with a winding walkway, a reflecting pool, and statues that seem to burst through the ground. Each of these statues has inscriptions of important people and places in the history of Civil Rights. In the center of the garden is a large bell (similar to the Liberty Bell), which rings during special occasions.

The garden features a nice landscape of flowers and plants (particularly in the summertime). Though it feels peaceful, there is definitely a feeling of gravity as you pass through the garden's gates. A wrought iron fence encapsulates the many pedestals. Visitors guide themselves along the path, stopping at the pedestals to read the inscriptions.

## RIPLEY'S BELIEVE IT OR NOT! MUSEUM
*(New York Ave & Boardwalk* ☎ *609.347.2001* ✆ *ripleys.com)*
Wherever there is a tourist town, there seems to be a **Ripley's Believe it or Not! Museum**. If you are driving towards a town with billboards for mini-golf, go-carts or roller coasters, and fudge shop after fudge shop, chances are you'll see a Ripley's. Atlantic City, Niagara Falls, Myrtle Beach, Wisconsin Dells, and many other towns have this attraction.

The Ripley's museum in Atlantic City is located directly on the Boardwalk by the ocean, sandwiched in between two large resort-hotels. It is just south of the Trump Taj Mahal, in a two story high building designed to look like it has just been whacked with a colorful wrecking ball, which has been decorated to look like Earth. The exhibits inside include a replica of the Jersey Devil skeleton, as well as some classic Ripley "artifacts" such as shrunken heads and unusually talented contortionists, and people who smoke cigarettes through their eyes.

Robert Leroy Ripley was born in 1890 in Santa Rosa, California. In 1908, he sold his first comic to LIFE magazine. After working for the San Francisco Chronicle and Boston's "The Globe", he decided to travel abroad. In 1918, he draws a cartoon featuring sports oddities, and one year later draws a comic called "Believe It Or Not!" From then on, Ripley traveled the world in search of oddities to write about and publish in his comic strips. In 1929 his strips earned syndication, read by millions worldwide. Ripley would work for radio, create short films and explore different avenues for his "Believe It or Not!" idea. In 1933, the first "Odditorium" museum opened in Chicago, followed shortly thereafter by San Diego and Dallas. In 1939 there was even an Odditorium opening in Times Square in New York City. In 1949, Robert Ripley collapsed on the set of his television show, and died shortly thereafter. The first Odditorium to open its doors in Atlantic City was in 1954 – but it closed in 1957.

Unlike many non-resort attractions, Ripley's *Believe It or Not!* Museum is open year-round, so even in the dead of winter you can walk through and enjoy the wonders. The entire museum tour is self-guided, and you can go through it in as little as half an hour, but you can take as long as you wish. ($$)

### DR. JONATHON PITNEY HOUSE

*(57 Shore Road* ☎ *609.569.1799* ✂ *pitneyhouse.com)* Before there was a resort town, and well before there were casinos, there was lonely Absecon Island, nothing more than a vast marshland surrounding a tiny village. Around 1820, after Dr. Jonathon Pitney graduated from medical school in New York, he made his way to the village, and set up his home there.

But Pitney had a dream. He envisioned a resort community on the Island, and a "Railroad to Nowhere" which would bring visitors from nearby towns into this would-be vacation paradise. It was Dr. Pitney's direct involvement in the establishment of a railway system to this city by the Atlantic Ocean (ultimately dubbed "Atlantic City" by the railroad company), which earned him the title "The Father of Atlantic City".

Pitney's house was originally built in 1799, and another wing was built (by Pitney himself) in 1848. In 1997, the house was restored and added to the National Register of Historic Places the following year. Today it occasionally functions as both a historical site and bed-and-breakfast.

Visitors may tour the Dr. Jonathon Pitney House in Absecon City, or spend one or more nights in one of their especially romantic and classically-appointed rooms and suites. The house and property are colonial in style, and guests are pampered with homemade breakfasts, as well as afternoon tea. The house is ideally suited for romance. Packages are available, if you are interested in a romantic getaway.

## ABSECON LIGHTHOUSE 🏛

*(31 S. Rhode Island Ave* ☎ *609.449.1360* ✆ *abseconlighthouse.org)*
Nestled in between otherwise unimpressive buildings, in a mostly residential area of Atlantic City, is the tallest lighthouse in New Jersey (and the third tallest in the United States). At 171 feet, the Absecon Lighthouse played an integral part in the development of the city, and of the Jersey Shore in general. It has recently been totally renovated and today serves as a hot historical attraction. The Absecon Lighthouse is named for the island on which it is situated, and is also one of the oldest structures in Atlantic City, built well before the Boardwalk.

Dr. Jonathon Pitney, considered by many to be the father of Atlantic City, cited numerous nautical disasters in Absecon Beach (the "Graveyard Inlet") as a reason to build a lighthouse. In 1854 the money was secured. Three years later, on January 15, 1857, the lighthouse was first lit. For years it helped seagoing vessels avoid the treachery of Absecon Beach. In 1933 the light was extinguished, and for a while the structure remained largely unused, except for some ceremonial events and mild tourism. In 1971, the lighthouse was placed on the National Register of Historic Places. After years of restorations and reorganizations, the tower itself finally opened to the public in 1999.

The Absecon Lighthouse is visible in the near distance from the northern end of the Boardwalk, particularly north of Showboat. Visitors may explore the gift shop, or climb the 228 steps to the viewing platform just below the lantern room. Though it is within walking distance of the Boardwalk, it is farther away than it seems, and you will probably enjoy it better by taking a short car or taxi ride, especially if you anticipate climbing to the top.

As east coasters, and New Englanders particularly, are well aware, lighthouses are big deals, both for tourism and for historical reasons. Absecon Lighthouse is among the best; but for those interested, a drive to the southern tip of New Jersey brings you to the Cape May Lighthouse, and a short drive north will bring you to the Barnegat Lighthouse. Together, these three sister lighthouses are among the most important in New Jersey. Today the Inlet Public/Private Association (IPPA) operates them. ($)

## LUCY THE ELEPHANT 🈲

*(9200 Atlantic Avenue* ☎ *609.823.6473* ✆ *lucytheelephant.com)* For those not familiar with the eclectic history of the Jersey Shore, Lucy the Elephant is an odd thing to explain. Given the many other monstrous and goofy architectural feats of today, Lucy may not be the most impressive thing ever built. But it has a certain quality that captures the history of the area quite well.

Lucy is in the town of Margate. If only for the sake of a mild thrill, this is definitely a hyped and must-see attraction, especially if you're traveling with young people or curio connoisseurs

So who is Lucy? She is a six-story tall elephant-shaped building (the largest "elephant" in the world). She is the quintessential roadside attraction: something totally pointless and somehow irresistible. She was initially built in 1881 as an attempt to sell real estate in the area (it has even been said that she was the area's first tourist attraction). She has been a real estate office, a summer home, a tavern, and a derelict landmark. In 1976, she was added to the National Register of Historic Places. The attraction is small, quaint and clean.

Aside from its size, it looks obviously artificial, like a papier-mâché creation, but that's the point. The parking is limited, but don't worry – you don't need to spend much time here to really enjoy it. Just check out the small museum, buy some gifts from the shop, and hop back in the car. The parking spaces for Lucy would be prime for beach-goers, but parking there is not allowed, unless you buy a tour ticket.

There is something totally adorable about Lucy the Elephant. She may very well be this area's very first roadside attraction, and has stood the test of time, even by Atlantic City standards. The exhibits inside highlight the history of this creation, with photographs, diagrams and a video presentation. The whole package is very kitschy and cute. Tours are guided, although the attraction itself is small and self-contained enough that it really doesn't need to be. She was actually modeled to look like an Indian elephant, which accounts for the carriage on her back. Also, despite the fact that she has a woman's name, she has tusks and is therefore not female.

The inside of Lucy is unexpected. As the tour begins, you climb up one of her hind legs in a narrow, winding staircase (like that of a lighthouse), and end up in a large room, reminiscent of a turn-of-the-century courthouse. You are in Lucy's torso - there is fine oak paneling and wood flooring, and everything is clean and tidy. There are small exhibits around the outer edge of this room. In this main room, you will watch a short video on the history of Lucy; her purpose and development. Then your guide will take you up on another staircase to the very top of Lucy where there is a truly great view of the beach and of surrounding Margate.

The tour is short; don't expect it to take longer than about 20 minutes (and the video takes up most of that time). If you're looking to kill an entire day, this attraction won't do it. But if you're anywhere around, this is honest, historical Jersey Shore tack that is sure to please anybody. Lucy's hours fluctuate based on the season. ($)

## OCEAN LIFE CENTER

*(800 N. New Hampshire* ☎ *609.348.2880* ✆ *oceanlifecenter.com)*
The resident aquarium in Atlantic City is the Ocean Life Center. Located in the Historic Gardner's Basin, the center features as many as eleven large tanks filled with various species of ocean life. There is even a special tank that allows visitors to reach in and touch some of the more unusual and exotic (but safe) animals.

The tanks of the aquarium each specialize in a particular kind of ocean environment. The "Fish of the New Jersey Coast" tank contains bluegill, weakfish, kingfish, nurse sharks, and more. The "Coral Reef" tank has varieties of sea life that live in a reef environment. Other tanks include "Seahorses & Shellfish", "Tropical Beauties", "Live Moon", "Jelly Fish", and more. The Center's inhabitants tend to rotate a bit due to species' availability. "Sea Sights & Sounds", "A Ships Bridge", and other permanent exhibits, as well as computer terminals loaded with marine life information, make for a well-rounded experience.

The Center is rather small, but packed with things to see and do. It consists of three floors, the main floor being the main aquarium area. Most of the exhibits are visible right from the front desk, which is also a gift shop. The second floor consists mainly of interactive exhibits and sets. The top floor – the roof of the center – has an outdoor portion that offers visitors a great 365-degree view of the Basin, the Marina District, and even the distant Boardwalk skyline.

The Ocean Life Center first opened in 1999. Access by car is the most convenient. It is located near the tip of the Gardner's Basin, surrounded almost completely by water. Directly on the other side of the water is the Trump Marina resort and the Farley State Marina. ($$)

## BALIC WINERY

*(6623 Harding Highway* ☎ *609.625.2166* ✆ *balicwinery.com)*
Mays Landing has had the winery in some form since the turn of
the 19th century, but wine entrepreneur Savo Balic purchased the
land in 1966, renaming it the Balic Winery. At 57 acres, Balic
Winery today bottles about 12,000 cases of wine per year, at 6-
12 bottles per case, one bottle at a time. The processing center
on the property itself caters mostly to the sales of wine and wine
tasting.

Tours are available; just ask for one. Visitors will note that
Balic Winery is a functional facility and does not as much cater
to tourists as do other vineyards in the area, such as Renault
Winery. If you are interested in wine, however, and want a quick
vineyard experience, Balic Winery is a good choice. For a more
elaborate daytrip or weekend trip, Renault offers a more comprehensive package.

## RENAULT WINERY

*(72 Bremen Avenue* ☎ *609.965.2111* ✆ *renaultwinery.com)*
Located in the New Jersey Pine Barrens about 35 miles away
from Atlantic City, the Renault Winery complex can be an entire
vacation destination in and of itself. The property features a hotel, several restaurants, a golf course, and a vineyard complete
with comprehensive tour and wine tasting. Ample space is available for weddings and conferences.

Louis Nicholas Renault first purchased the land on which
the winery sits in 1864. After having some bad luck with his
vineyards in France and California, he moved his operation to
Egg Harbor and proceeded to win many awards for the wine
produced there. During Prohibition, the winery was sold to John
D'Agostino who sold wine on a limited basis. Since then it has
exchanged hands several times, until Joseph P. Milza, who currently owns and operates the entire resort, finally acquired it.

Stepping onto the main vineyard complex today feels very much like stepping into a small French vineyard. The **House of Renault** is the centerpiece of the winery, made of dark wood and surrounded by a French-influenced garden. The entry doors for the main tour are massive wooden structures. The small garden surrounding the house has a few gazebos for relaxing and gathering, and a stream of water flows throughout, with walking bridges crossing it in places. There is also a gift shop on the site as well as a place to buy Renault wine. The guided tour focuses on the wine processing, and includes history of the vineyard ("how could such a vineyard have wound up in Egg Harbor Township?"). Your tour guide will bring you into the real working rooms in the various stages of grape harvesting, fermentation, and distribution. At the end of the tour, Renault gives you the opportunity to taste some select wines.

The **Renault Gourmet Restaurant** has been touted as one of the most romantic places to eat in the Atlantic City area. Across the complex is the **Tuscany House**, a small hotel that caters to guests of the vineyard and nearby golf course. The rooms, like the rest of the resort, are reminiscent of fine European styles. Inside is **Joseph's Restaurant**, which offers classy décor and a diverse menu.

**The Vineyard Golf** is a brand new addition to the Renault complex, opened in 2004, which really transforms the complex from just a hotel and vineyard to a complete vacation resort. This unique course offers on some holes a very nice view of the vast vineyard property. The course is full-size, covering about 7,000 yards on the complex. They offer memberships as well as a tee-at-a-time option.

Guests wishing to make Renault their destination of choice have the option of several vacation packages that may include rooms, vineyard tours, gourmet dinners, and golf tee times. Call the main Renault Winery number for more information. This is definitely a must-see attraction in south Jersey. It is family-friendly for a vineyard, but there isn't much to do for those not into wine, golf, or fine dining. At one point the Renault Winery was the largest producer of wine in the United States, and it remains one of the oldest operating vineyards in the country today.

## THE NOYES MUSEUM

*(Lily Lake Rd* ☎ *609.652.8848* ✆ *noyesmuseum.org)* Entrepreneurs Fred and Ethel Noyes had first hoped to open a fine art museum in south Jersey as early as 1974, when their sale of the History Towne of Smithville to ABC provided enough money to start pre-planning. After Mrs. Noyes death in 1979, the museum's future rested on the shoulders of the Mr. and Mrs. Fred Winslow Noyes foundation. The museum finally opened in 1983.

The Noyes Museum is directly adjacent to the Edgar B. Forsythe National Wildlife Refuge, in an idyllic location. It is a small museum, but full; it focuses primarily on folk art and craft (art created with practical purpose), particularly American art. The museum has a permanent collection as well as temporary exhibits. Among other exhibits, it has a large collection of hunting decoys as well as a selection of cottage arts, such as quilts, woodworking, and pottery. There is also a special section dedicated to art on display from local schools.

The museum also has a shop on the premises, where you can purchase collectible art and other exhibit-related memorabilia. There is also adequate space for corporate or private functions. Membership options are also available. ($$)

*Established in 1915, the **Atlantic City Jitney** is the oldest privately-funded public transportation system in the country.*

# Parks and Recreation

The Jersey Shore is host to a wide variety of outdoor activities. However, most other shore points revolve around swimming or summertime activities. Atlantic City is unique in this aspect – it has sports and recreational activities of all sorts, which range from the standard summertime fare to truly unique retreats and even wildlife experiences and education centers.

In addition to opportunities within the city, some significant natural and recreational activities are a short drive away from the city. State and Federal parks are abundant in New Jersey, and two of the most important ones are located just outside Atlantic City.

## EDWIN B. FORSYTHE NATIONAL WILDLIFE REFUGE

*(Great Creek Road* ☎ *609.652.1665)* Much of the Jersey Shore (particularly the south Shore) is uninhabitable marsh. For this reason, arriving at various Shore points, including Atlantic City, requires first traversing large land masses of flat, marshy landscape and shallow lakes. Only the very edges – just along the ocean – have been developed.

The Edwin B. Forsythe National Wildlife Refuge is about 40,000 acres representative of this type of coastal wetlands landscape. The refuge is largely inaccessible; however, there is an 8-mile expansive donation-funded vehicle "safari" within the area that gives a good impression of the land. The refuge serves mainly as a resting place for migratory birds (like portions of New York City's Gateway National Recreation Area). If you are a bird watcher, you will feel particularly at home here. There are "patches" of the reserve located at strategic points just north of Atlantic City. The main vehicular entrance is accessible via

Route 9 Just north of Atlantic City (take White Horse Pike to 9 North).

The Refuge is part of the New Jersey Coastal Heritage Trail. This series of parks and natural environments runs down the Jersey Shore from Sandy Hook to Cape May, and then wraps a little bit around the southern tip of the state. It is meant to be a trail for vehicles to follow down the shore. The trail itself is not one particular "thing", but rather a collection of independent federal and state run sites that have been grouped in this manner. In other words, if you are driving down the Jersey Shore, you are exploring the Coastal Heritage Trail.

## WHARTON STATE FOREST AND BATSTO VILLAGE

*(4110 Nesco Road* ☎  *609.561.0024)* Wharton State Forest, approximately twenty miles away from Atlantic City, is the largest state forest in New Jersey. It is not directly on the Jersey Shore (unlike the Edwin B. Forsythe National Wildlife Refuge), but it is close and is a stark contrast to the Shore's natural landscape. Consisting of about 110,000 acres, Wharton covers ground in three counties: Burlington, Camden, and Atlantic. It was named after Joseph Wharton, who purchased large portions of land in the area during the late 1800s, with the intent to reap financial benefits by using the land for its agriculture and commercial assets. But Wharton passed away before any real damage to the forest was done. New Jersey purchased the land in the mid-1950s, and today the New Jersey Division of Parks and Forestry manages it. Officially, Wharton State Forest is part of the New Jersey Pinelands area.

Driving into Wharton State Forest, especially from the heavily populated Jersey Shore area, with eight-or-more-lane highways, seems like an unusual and sudden jolt. In a matter of feet, the road changes from a massive highway to a mere 2-lane country road, deeply shrouded by tall trees on either side. Signs from the Garden State Parkway and Atlantic City Expressway point to the appropriate exit to reach the forest, but don't expect it to be right around the corner.

Though most of the forest remains in its natural state, some areas within it have been developed both recreationally and commercially. There are year-round campsites scattered all around the area, particularly near Crowley Landing, Atsion, and Batsto Village. Route 542 and 206 are the two main thruways into and out of Wharton, but there are dozens of unpaved roads that take you as far into the forest as you are willing to go. There are hiking trails, natural picnic and swimming areas, and horseback riding trails.

The most significant of these is Batsto Village, the principal purchase of Joseph Wharton, made in 1876. Originally, however, Charles Read created Batsto Iron Works on the Batsto River in 1766. It changed hands several times since then (eventually landing on Wharton), while always maintaining its industrial iron-and-glassmaking core. Today the buildings are preserved, and visitors are free to explore the village on foot and even walk into several dozen buildings to learn about the industry of the day. Visitors will notice the buildings in Batsto Village have a historic cabin look to them. The bridge over Batsto Lake offers a great view of the small, serene lake.

If you are interested in seeing Batsto Village but want to get a taste of Wharton State Forest along the way, 542 off the Garden State Parkway (going north, take exit 50 north to 542) will take you along the southern edge of the forest, a very wooded drive, and past the water at Crowley Landing, where recreational boating is allowed. ($)

## BEL HAVEN CANOES AND KAYAKS

*(1227 Route 542* ☎ *609.965.2205* ☝ *belhavencanoe.com)* For the athletic nature lover, the New Jersey Pinelands area offers out-

door water canoeing and kayaking activities close to Atlantic City. Bel Haven, in the Wharton State Forest area, offers options for adventurous souls such as canoeing, kayaking and more. Explore the Oswego, Mullica, Wading, or Batsto rivers either in large groups or by yourself. You and your group are generally free to explore the river on your own, and you may even stop at various points to explore. The rivers are generally calm, though there may be some rougher sections on occasion.

Prices are per canoe per day, but tours can run anywhere from a few hours to several days (nearby campsites are available along the various river routes). This activity requires a certain amount of athletic ability and a basic knowledge of canoeing or kayaking. However, on occasion, guided tours may be avail able for certain routes and seasons. Canoes are advised for two people, whereas kayaks are suitable for one. ($/$$$)

### HISTORIC GARDNER'S BASIN

*(New Hampshire & Parkside Ave)* Tucked away in a small corner of Atlantic City that seems out of the way from everything else, is historic Gardner's Basin. Modeled after a New England fishing village, this small, gated area is a real unexpected and pleasant surprise. Most people traveling there are destined for either one of several privately-owned Atlantic City cruises, or the family-friendly Ocean Life Center, but the entire area is a real treat and features several different unique opportunities (and one heck of a nice view). And better yet, most of these attractions, even the boating excursions, can be open year round (but call ahead during the winter months).

Gardner's Basin is located on a small peninsula immediately across from Trump Marina. It is near the northern end of the Boardwalk (after it wraps around Absecon Island, north of Show-boat). Enter the area by car via New Hampshire Avenue. The Basin, named after former Atlantic City Mayor John H.

Gardner, was actually the location of the first hotels in Atlantic City. A majority of the surrounding water area is devoted to various marinas - some of which have vessels that operate public tours and charters.

The area has had its ups and downs over the years, much like the rest of Atlantic City. However, the recent renovation of Gardner's Basin allowed for the new **Ocean Life Center**, as well as several major renovations to the area. Now visitors can eat lunch, take a boat cruise, explore oceanography, or just walk around this unique village. You may see people fishing off one of the three shores of the peninsula, or snap some photos of the Marina District, or just-over-the-bridge Brigantine.

Gardner's Basin is a small but pretty area, scattered with fishing-village-style buildings. They look very much like small country houses that have been converted into even smaller restaurants, bars, or shops. Parking (and limited boat docking) is free to visitors, so feel free to walk around a little bit.

From the main parking lot, the first establishment you'll notice is the **Back Bay Ale House** (☎ 609.449.0006). The exterior looks small, and when you look inside, the interior is even smaller. A small bar mostly takes up the main area, but food is served both inside and on a patio outside. Also nearby is Back Bay Ice Cream, which serves all the classic cold treats, including snacks and gelato.

The **Flying Cloud Café** (☎ 609.345.8222) has a great waterfront location, where you can enjoy a nice selection of specialty seafood dishes, including a raw bar. The **Lobster Shanty** (☎ 609.344.9030), with a great view of the Gardner's Basin marina, allows you to dine on lobster while you watch boats move in and out of the area.

All restaurants in the Gardner's Basin area are quick eats and very casual. The hours vary seasonally and by establishment so it's a good idea to check ahead of time by calling (although no reservations are required). Expect lots of Atlantic City locals as well as tourists. Children are welcome here, and it can be especially rewarding after an afternoon of exploring the Ocean Life Center.

## BOAT CRUISES AND CHARTERS

*(New Hampshire & Parkside)* If boating is your thing, there is an entire culture in New Jersey devoted to the boating industry. Marinas are abundant all down the Jersey Shore (it's a very big business) and both pleasure and commercial boaters make use of the various facilities. As a result, there is much nautical traffic in and around Gardner's Basin, from small boats to fishing vessels to multimillion-dollar yachts. For tourists, Gardner's Basin is the debarkation point for various boating excursions in and around Atlantic City. The tours vary from sightseeing to fishing expeditions to charters in and around the Atlantic City area. Some of these companies have walk-up opportunities, while others require a special reservation.

If you are just interested in a general tour of Atlantic City, **Cruisn 1** (☎ 609.347.7600) is your main choice. They offer cruise options that sail at various hours of the day in the summertime, including a Harbor Tour. Wintertime cruises are available by charter.

If you want to do some fishing, you may be able to do it from the shorelines of the Gardner's Basin area, or you could check out one of the three fishing cruises. **Shore Bet Fishing** (☎ 609.345.4077) offers half-day trips as well as nighttime fishing. Or you can book a seat on the **High Roller** (☎ 609.348.3474), a large pontoon boat. Though some of these companies may be available for private charters, **Atlantus Charters** (☎ 609.408.3564) makes that a priority - you can even book scuba diving or other special requests with them.

## EXTREME WINDSURFING

*(7079      Black      Horse      Pike     ☎    609.641.4445
✆  extremewindsurfing.com)* Lakes Bay, located on the southern tip
of Atlantic City and accessible via Black Horse Pike, is a favorite
local place for water sports. As the lake is part of the larger marsh
that comprises much of the Jersey Shore's coastal wetlands, it is
shallow and motor-powered boats have limited access – though
are seldom seen. This combined with almost consistent wind, is
an ideal place for windsurfing or kite surfing.

Extreme Windsurfing, located right next to Lakes Bay and
the Hampton Inn, is well-equipped for both beginning and advanced windsurfers. In addition to sales and rentals of all types of
equipment and accessories, it also offers lessons on the sport. If
you are interested in purchasing equipment, Extreme Windsurfing allows you to try out the latest equipment before you decide
to make a purchase. Windsurfers and kite surfers should be in
good physical shape, and have a basic knowledge of the sport.
Lessons are available, and you must sign a comprehensive waiver
before taking to the bay. The facilities on-site include the Hampton Inn, a small beach, storage, snack bar, and other amenities.

## MARINE MAMMAL STRANDING CENTER

*(3625 Brigantine Blvd. ☎   609.266.0537 ✆  mmsc.org)* In 1978,
the Marine Mammal Stranding Center was established to help
distressed and stranded marine life in the area. Sea turtles, dol-
phins, whales, and other sea mammals have been assisted here,
sometimes as many as 175 per year. Since opening, the center
has rescued over 2,500 animals of various kinds. Originally headquartered in Gardner's Basin, the center is the only such facility
in New Jersey, and has a federal and state permit to assist
stranded mammals.

Visitors are allowed limited access to tour the facilities for a
small donation. The actual rehabilitation center is off-limits, but

visitors can still see much of the facility, including a small museum/gallery (the "Sea Life Educational Center"). There is also an on-site gift shop featuring logo shirts, CDs, and videos. Summertime hours are generally steady, but it is strongly recommended that you call ahead, as access to the facility tends to vary greatly year-round, but especially in the winter. The center operates on volunteer services and donations. On occasion, aquatic excursions may be offered (call well in advance).

*The largest casino in Atlantic City – the Bally's complex – is larger than the largest casino in Las Vegas.*

# Shopping

The recent major overhaul of Atlantic City entertainment centers includes the addition of several new shopping centers. Area resorts are shifting their gears towards more non-gambling establishments, and malls so far seem to be the general direction of this trend.

The malls and shopping areas listed here are in and around the Atlantic City area. Some will require a short drive, while others may be easily accessible from certain points on the Boardwalk. However, all of them have a wide selection of shops. Shopaholics will probably find themselves at home in any one of these establishments (note that resorts may have their own shopping facilities, descriptions of which are located elsewhere in this book.)

## ATLANTIC CITY OUTLETS

*(1801 Baltic Avenue* ☎ *609.343.0081* ⌐ *acoutlets.com)* Like shopping but hate the high price tag on your favorite name-brand items? Let's do some outlet shopping!

In recent years, Atlantic City has been trying to attract a crowd that is not expressly gamblers. A good way to do this is to create an outlet mall. Those who love to shop will really appreciate this new outdoor mall, located off the Boardwalk, directly across from Caesars Atlantic City and Bally's Park Place.

The Walk is entirely outdoors – so you'll need to have your raincoat/sweater/whatever if you want to spend any time there in inclement weather. All the standards are represented: **Gap, J. Crew**, **Banana Republic**, **Mikasa**, **Guess**, and many more are on the way. The Walk is regularly expanding with new stores. Who knows what stores the future will bring, though for the merchants it looks bright! It also contains lots of clean public spaces, restaurants such as **Subway Sandwiches** and **Star-**

**bucks**, and everything you would expect from any other quality outlet mall. The Walk is not in an enclosed area; it is a series of buildings compacted into a small section of town.

Additionally, walking along the street from shop to shop gives visitors an abbreviated history of Miss America. How? Each section is dedicated to a certain decade in Miss America's history. Engraved in the sidewalk, and on nearby signs, are biographies, pictures, and other information about past Miss America winners (if you enjoy Miss America, you may want to check out the nearby Sheraton Hotel's Miss America showcase near the hotel lobby, which features dresses, crowns, and more).

This is a great outlet mall; rivaling other top-notch shopping centers across the country, and a worthy addition to Atlantic City.

### SIGANOS PLAZA

*(1700 Boardwalk* ☎ *609.646.2292)* A unique mix of shops and restaurants, Siganos Plaza is a small strip mall located on the Boardwalk. The bright architecture of the plaza is immediately recognizable, and the colorful shops are just as eclectic on the inside as they are on the outside.

On the southern edge of the mall (next to the pedestrian walkway into Claridge) is the unique Mediterranean restaurant **Opa**. The mall also has **Original Philly Steak**, **China One**, and **Lo Presti Pizza** for quicker bites to eat. If you have a sweet tooth, **Kandyland** has a nice assortment of tantalizing sweets. Also, **Double Rainbow Ice Cream and Coffee Café** sells just what the name suggests.

Cartoon collectibles are abundant at **Toon In**. For the sports nut, **Sports Collection** has all sorts of licensed team memorabilia and apparel (hats and jerseys). **Wacky Bear** is a unique idea – children (and adults alike) are permitted to create their own stuffed animals by stuffing and dressing a selection of adorable animals. **Spotlight** offers women's clothing, from casual wear to sleepwear to some cosmetic jewelry and accessories. **Tiki Liki** also sells clothes and different kinds of beach apparel and accessories. **Lady of Leisure** sells all sorts of women's accessories such as handbags, jewelry, and more. **Natural Health Centers** offers a unique and strangely popular aqua massage; somebody lies down under a thick wall of rubber while water spray nozzles massage you up and down. If you like magnets, then you'll love **Magnetism**, a store devoted entirely to covering up your refrigerator with decorative items. Finally, for your basic magazine and candy needs, Siganos Plaza is topped off with a **Newsstand**.

## DOWNTOWN ATLANTIC CITY

*(Northern Atlantic Avenue)* Atlantic Avenue is the main non-resort shopping district of Atlantic City. In particular, the strip between Trump Taj Mahal and the Atlantic City Expressway is home to many local shops. Grocery stores, mini malls, pawnshops, gold/jewelry dealers, and a few restaurants are packed into this small area, which don't seem to be related to the nearby resorts. This is part of the "real" Atlantic City.

As these are all independent stores, there is no single opening or closing time, though many seem to close before dark. These shops are all located within a short walk to one of several resorts, but its best to explore this area during the day, when a lot of people are present (and before the Atlantic City "nightlife" crowd takes over). Overall, it is a shopping area with local flavor.

## FRALINGER'S SALT WATER TAFFY

*(Two locations on the Boardwalk in Atlantic City: At Tennessee Avenue and at Bally's Park Place.)* Mr. Bradley had no name for his unique taffy treats (a chewy mix of corn syrup and sugar), so he let his Boardwalk patrons call it whatever they wished. On one particu-

lar day in August 1883 (the story goes), he was selling his taffy as usual. But a nasty storm blew salt water all over poor Mr. Bradley's stand. After the storm passed, a young girl ordered from Mr. Bradley some of his taffy, which had been drenched in the ocean's salt water. "Don't you mean 'Salt Water Taffy'?" Mr. Bradley asked the girl. Mr. Fralinger – interested in opening a taffy stand of his own - was standing nearby and overheard the remark, and the name "Salt Water Taffy" was born.

Those who have enjoyed Salt Water Taffy in candy stores across the country may not know that this treat – hardly salty or watery – is an Atlantic City original. Fralinger's Salt Water Taffy popularized the treat after he opened up his own shop in 1885. Today the shops are full-fledged candy stores, but the taffy selection is extensive. Choose from many, many different flavors, mix and match your candy pieces, or buy a box with a pre-sorted mix.

Fralinger's has two locations on the Atlantic City Boardwalk today. There are also locations in nearby Ocean City and Cape May. Those visiting from afar may also order taffy online at www.fralingers.com or by calling 1-800-93-TAFFY. Though many companies may produce Salt Water Taffy today, Fralinger's is "officially" the original.

## HISTORIC SMITHVILLE 🚇

*(1 New York Road ☎ 609.652.7777 ⬧ smithvillenj.com)* In 1787 there was only Smithville Inn. Built on a common stagecoach route and run by James Baremore, the Inn eventually became a popular resting place for weary travelers, as not many houses or other establishments existed in the area. But, as the years went by and more area commerce arose, the need for an Inn at this spot diminished, until the property finally was abandoned at around the turn of the 20th century. In the early 1950s Fred and Ethel Noyes purchased the structure and restored it into a restaurant,

and the seven acres surrounding the Inn would eventually become known as The Towne of Historic Smithville.

Today, the seven-acre "town", a National Historic Landmark, is a re-creation of what an east coast village looked like in the 1700s. Cobblestone streets align village buildings, a Village Green, complete with gazebo, a small lake, and nearly every building is packed with handcrafts and thingamajigs for sale. Many of the buildings, purchased by the Noyes, were from sites all over this part of New Jersey. Historic Smithville is a must-see for anybody and can be a particularly fun afternoon for families with children.

The collection of shops is eclectic and shopping here can be very relaxing and enjoyable. Stores include **The Candle Shoppe**, **The Christmas Shoppe**, **Cozy Fireside Treasures**, **The Jewelry Box**, **Pocket Full of Posies**, **Country Folk**, and dozens more, including places to eat, from a quick bite to a lavish multi-course dinner. Aside from shopping, visitors may enjoy paddle boating on the lake, a mini train ride; a remote-controlled boat course, a carousel, and an old-time arcade. Although Historic Smithville is open year-round, some of the other attractions are only available during the warmer months. **The Smithville Inn**, of course, is still there. It serves as a meeting and banquet facility. Weddings here are common, but they also serve lunch, dinner, and occasionally brunch.

Historic Smithville also has a small hospitable lodging facility available. **The Colonial Inn** (615 East Moss Mill Road, Smithville, NJ, 609.748.8999, colonialinnsmithville.com) is a bed and breakfast-style located directly on the grounds. It is open year-round and features eight rooms, some of which overlook the lake. The rooms are decorated to reflect the period. Rates include private bathrooms and standard hotel amenities. However, though Historic Smithville is very family-friendly, small children are not encouraged not to stay at The Colonial Inn.

Throughout the year, Historic Smithville redecorates itself with holiday themes. Throughout August and September, it is host to special events, such as concerts and sidewalk sales. One of the largest events is Oktoberfest, where arts and crafts abound. During this time, there is also a "Haunted Train Ride" on weekends. For the holidays, there is a "Christmas Train Ride" and Santa Claus himself may even make a personal appearance.

Historic Smithville has enough to see and do to occupy an entire day, particularly during the summertime. Its small size and themed nature are second only to its impeccable charm. Near a city with big lights and flashy facades, the quaint and beautiful Smithville is an absolute breath of fresh air, and a must-see.

*For a brief period, Steve Wynn's Golden Nugget chain had a resort in Atlantic City. It is where the Atlantic City Hilton sits today.*

# Clubs and Nightlife

Atlantic City is an up-all-night kind of place. The casinos are open 24-hours a day, 7 days a week, which naturally gives rise to other possibilities of nightlife. Like Las Vegas, Atlantic City is famous for its after-hours entertainment opportunities. While some major resort hotels offer generally safe, upscale clubbing experiences (particularly **Casbah** at Trump Taj Mahal, **Mixx** at the Borgata, and **The Wave** at Trump Marina), the city itself has numerous other ways to kill time before the sun rises.

*Atlantic City's nightlife is strictly for adults!* Even the resorts' clubs and bars are meant for those over 21 (sometimes over 18). Be warned that children should not venture from the resorts during the nighttime hours. Because of the vast dichotomy between resortland and cityland, mere steps away from the casino's entrance could bring any unsuspecting wanderer into an area that he or she would prefer not enter. Atlantic City streets off the resort properties are incredibly diverse. You may find yourself one moment under the glitzy umbrella of a resort, and in the next moment on a deserted city street. Keep your wits about you.

That being said, if you're up to experiencing Atlantic City's nightlife, this section describes some of the wide range of entertainment and activities available, besides gambling, during the nighttime hours. Atlantic City nights begin at approximately 8-9PM, and facilities will close between about 2-3AM (except for casinos, of course).

## CASINOS

Every casino in Atlantic City, whether it is on the Boardwalk or in the Marina District, is open 24 hour a day, 7 days a week. Casino gambling is by far the #1 nighttime entertainment option in Atlantic City, and very likely on the entire Jersey Shore. Few other venues across the country have such a wide operating schedule, and will be crowded even in the wee hours of the morning.

A gaming day in Atlantic City starts at about 6:00AM and runs until 5:59AM the following morning. No matter what time of year you intend on visiting Atlantic City, and no matter which resort you visit, and what time of day you go, there will always, *always* be activity on the casino floor.

But which casino is right for you? That is entirely your choice. Many people gamble only in the resort in which they are staying, whereas others casino-hop across the Boardwalk. Many people are devoted to one single players' club, whereas others have thick wallets with club cards from each of the resorts. One of the best features of Atlantic City, of course, is the freedom to move around with ease.

## RESORT BARS AND LOUNGES

Every casino resort in Atlantic City has at least one late-night bar, and most have at least three or four. If you're in a resort, you're never more than a few steps from at least one place to relax and drink. Sometimes they are swanky, sometimes casual, but they are almost always open late, and almost always busy. For more information on a particular bar or lounge with a resort, see the resort's section elsewhere in this book.

## RESORT CLUBS

A few casino resorts feature an on-site nightclub. These are generally glossy, inoffensive places that can be enjoyed by young and old alike. **Casbah** in Trump Taj Mahal and **Mixx** in Borgata are among the best, but **The Quarter** at Tropicana and **The Pier Shops at Caesars** each have places to keep the night young. See the resort's listing elsewhere in this book for more information.

## CLUBS AT THE QUARTER

*(At Tropicana)* During weekend nights (past 11pm) Tropicana's Quarter becomes a real club-goers paradise. Many of the dining establishments – quiet by day – convert into nightclubs, and the younger local New Jersey crowds pack into the streets of "Old Havana" as tightly as they would during the busiest weekends at Seaside Heights. The result: a loud crowd of crazy teens and twenty-something adults too young to gamble. Love it or hate it, this influx of young people has made Tropicana one of the must-go local places for a much younger crowd than is typical in Atlantic City.

## 40/40 CLUB

*(2120 Atlantic Ave* ☎ *609.449.4040* ✆ *the4040club.com)* Jay Z.'s chain of bars and clubs has a home at the Atlantic City Outlets. This sports bar and lounge is designed to be a hip, posh place to sit and relax. The modern interior look has the feel of a contemporary casino restaurant, if a bit more claustrophobic. A wide range of drinks are available, as well as a full continental food menu (burgers and the like). They can also host a variety of private parties. ($)

## CLUB TRU

*(9 S. Martin Luther King Jr. Blvd* ☎ *609.347.3500* ✆ *clubtru.com)* For locals as well as tourists, Club Tru is one of Atlantic City's more popular nighttime entertainment spots. It has the organization of a resort – visitors who enter can choose between different attractions located directly on the property. The club requires an admission charge, which allows access to the various facilities within. The charge varies from day to day and depending on your situation (ladies, for example, sometimes get free admission before midnight).

The indoor complex is huge – three floors full of various nightlife attractions. The main attractions are the dance halls, **Club Tru** and **Studio Six**. Here, the lights flash and the sweaty pulse of DJ-spinned music rocks the house all through the night. The **Tru Energy Bar** has caffeine-infused alcoholic beverages to keep your heart rate up. For a more relaxed visitor, **Joe's Sports Bar** on the ground floor is a place to have a beer and relax, while still being close to the action. For a more upscale drink surrounding, the **Perfect 10 Martini Lounge** and **4c's VIP Lounge** cater to the more expensive drinks and more relaxing surroundings. But remember – it is still a club, so just about anywhere you decide to drink is going to have a nighttime pulse.

Club Tru is also directly connected – through an inside corridor – to the **Surfside Resort Hotel** (18 South Mt. Vernon Avenue 609.347.7873). This is a smaller hotel with 50 rooms, ranging from standard size to a penthouse suite, each with an individual style. The reasonable room rates and close proximity to the Boardwalk and Club Tru makes this a good spot if you plan on experiencing a lot of Atlantic City's nightlife. The hotel stands well on its own, with on-property establishments such as an outdoor pool and sun deck and various drinking establishments.

**STRIP CLUBS**

Strip clubs in Atlantic City tend to be popular places for locals as well as travelers visiting the casinos. Don't expect the New York City or Las Vegas showiness of these clubs. These are generally small, congested places filled mostly with men and a few scantily clad women. Cover charges are almost unavoidable. Generally the sport in these facilities is male bonding coupled with girl watching. Information about strip clubs in Atlantic City is available through several of the area's local publications.

*The only property in the original Monopoly game that is not in Atlantic City is Marvin Gardens − and it is misspelled in the game (the real spelling is "Marven Gardens", named for being on the border of Margate and Ventnor).*

# Select Restaurants

Aside from the restaurants located within the resorts themselves, Atlantic City boasts a wide range of dining options, from casual to fine dining and everything in between. This section details a few of the more popular restaurants, both in an out of the resorts, around the city. *Please note that there are many Atlantic City restaurants not described here, including restaurants described elsewhere in this book.*

As is to be expected, Atlantic City restaurants tend to open and close, change names or cuisines at the drop of a hat. Following is a list of select restaurants in the area. It is highly recommended that you contact any of these establishments to confirm availability. Prices are indicated as follows:

| | | |
|---|---|---|
| $$$ | - | Expensive (More than $20 per entrée) |
| $$ | - | Moderate ($10 - $20 per entrée) |
| $ | - | Inexpensive ($10 or less per entrée) |

## ANGELO'S FAIRMOUNT TAVERN

*(2300 Fairmont Ave ☝ angelosfairmounttavern.com ☎ 609.344.2439)* This classis Italian restaurant, which opened in 1935, features typical Italian cuisine in a casual dining setting. Angelo's also offers a banquet hall suitable for weddings or other special occasions. ($$)

## ATLANTIC CITY BAR & GRILL

*(1219 Pacific Avenue ☎ 609.348.8080 ☝ acbarandgrill.com)* The Atlantic City Bar & Grill began as a pizzeria in the 1980s. Today, this casual and popular restaurant serves up a mix of greasy spoon foods and finer seafood. ($$)

## RUTH'S CHRIS STEAKHOUSE

*(2020 Atlantic Ave ☎ 609.344.5833 ☝ ruthschris-atlanticcity.com)*

One of chain of upscale steakhouses, the Ruth's Chris Steakhouse is located within the Atlantic City Outlets. Their major menu items are steak dishes with the standard wine and ambience. ($$)

## DOCK'S OYSTER HOUSE 🏆

*(2405 Atlantic Avenue ☎ 609.345.0092 ✆ docksoysterhouse.com)* Having opened in 1897, Dock's Oyster House is an Atlantic City institution that features seafood in a friendly but fine dining environment. ($$)

## THE VIRGINIA CITY BUFFET

*(At Bally's Wild Wild West Casino)* The Virginia City Buffet is designed to look like a country home's back porch. There are several "stations" that mimic a mini-mall of food. From **John Wang's Asian Cuisine** to the **Remember the Alamode** dessert station, the tongue-in-cheek humor of Bally's is carried throughout. You can even get a full steak cooked to order. On busy weekends, expect to make a reservation up to several hours in advance. ($$)

## FLYING CLOUD CAFE

*(800 N. New Hampshire Ave ☎ 609.345.8222 ✆ atlanticcityflyingcloud.com)* Very inexpensive, very casual, and very unique, this dockside greasy spoon has bar and comfort foods (wings, chicken tenders, oysters, etc). Located in Gardner's Basin, Flying Cloud has a local feel and features an outdoor deck and occasional live music. (Seasonal) ($)

## IRISH PUB & INN

*(164 St. James Place ☎ 609.344.9063 ✆ theirishpub.com)* This extremely casual bar and restaurant (which also has a branch in Philadelphia) features inexpensive food, Irish drinks and snacks.

There is also a tiny Inn (i.e. room accommodations) but the main draw is the bar itself. Unfortunately, the location is rather inconveniently out of the way from most Atlantic City resorts, stuck between Uptown and Midtown. ($)

## KNIFE & FORK INN

*(Atlantic & Pacific Ave* ☎ *609.344.1133* ✆ *knifeandforkinn.com)* Originally built in 1912 as a secret club during Prohibition, the upscale casual Knife & Fork Inn is a famous local establishment serving seafood and steak. The recently renovated dining rooms reflect the classic Prohibition-era styles, and the wine list is extensive. ($$$)

## OLD HOMESTEAD

*(At the Borgata* ✆ *theborgata.com)* As with the rest of Borgata, the Old Homestead Steakhouse is simply the best steakhouse in Atlantic City. The prices are steep at this upscale establishment, but the selections are wide and the classic Borgata service is top-notch. If steak is your thing, and Atlantic City is your place, then Old Homestead will be quite a hard cut to follow, indeed. ($$$)

## OPA

*(1743 Boardwalk* ☎ *609.344.0094* ✆ *opa1.com)* This hip restaurant, located on the Boardwalk, features upscale casual Mediterranean-style dining. The cuisine and ambience is one of the few non-resort restaurants on the Boardwalk that serves non-pizza-style foods. ($$)

## SPECCHIO 🟥

*(At the Borgata* ✆ *theborgata.com)* The upscale Specchio has the rare Atlantic City honor of being a AAA Four Diamond restaurant award winner. As the only restaurant to hold this title, it offers very contemporary Italian cuisine, a high price tag, and

consistently busy clientele. Chef Luke Palladino has created an eclectic Italian menu that includes, soups, pastas, seafood (including lobster) and steaks. ($$$)

## TUN TAVERN

*(2 Ocean Wy* ☎ *609.347.7800* ⌖ *tuntavern.com)* Part of the Sheraton Hotel building, Tun Tavern is an upscale casual establishment that serves steak and seafood. It is particularly noteworthy for its on-property brewery. ($$$)

## WHITE HOUSE SUB SHOP 🏚

*(2301 Arctic Avenue* ☎ *609.345.8599)* This landmark casual restaurant, perhaps the most famous restaurant in Atlantic City, has been visited by the likes of such celebrities as Frank Sinatra. Though a bit of a dive, the large submarine sandwiches (and particularly the bread) are the best in New Jersey, and perhaps even of the Northeast. ($)

## WONDER BAR

*(3701 Sunset Avenue* ☎ *609.345.8599* ⌖ *wonderbarac.com)* Featuring seafood and sandwiches, this fine dining establishment is located on the water, with an open patio during the warm months. The "Sunset Room" offers nice views of a waterway thoroughfare. ($$/$$$)

*George C. Tilyou operated both Steeplechase Park in Coney Island and Steeplechase Pier in Atlantic City.*

# Recommendations

There are many other sources to find Atlantic City information, and other places to stay during your trip. The following sources will provide additional information to help you better plan your next Atlantic City (or Jersey Shore) vacation.

## TOP RESORTS

**The Borgata** is the newest resort in Atlantic City, and also one of the best casino resorts outside of Las Vegas. It is classy, expensive, with a wide array of entertainment and dining choices. Its location in the Marina District is a bit of a deterrent, but it's a place that any visitor to Atlantic City should behold.

**Trump Taj Mahal** While I'll be the first to admit that Donald Trump's ideas about style aren't much better than tacky, this is one place where all the pieces seem to fit together. Trump Taj is a large and splendid resort, with many on-site amenities and a gargantuan gaming floor.

**Tropicana** isn't particularly classy, but its themed gaming areas, impressive shopping, wide variety of eating and drinking options, and a nice spa make it an extremely popular "younger-crowd" resort. I enjoy the ambience because it reminds me of the friendlier themed casinos along the Las Vegas strip.

## TOP ATTRACTIONS

**The Quarter** Tropicana's Havana-themed shopping and dining center mimics that of the best Las Vegas themed malls. While much smaller, it is packed with kitschy (and nicer) shops, a wide range of dining, a comedy club, a movie theater, several night-clubs, and a lot of young New Jersey club-goers on the weekends.

**The Pier Shops at Caesars** The newest (and by far the most contemporary) new pier attraction is filled with shopping and dining choices. While a bit on the expensive side, the pier offers a more upscale experience, and older crowds than the Quarter.

**The Pools of Bally's and Harrah's** Atlantic City's climate and easy ocean access make world-class pool facilities unlikely, but as Atlantic City spas and pools go, Bally's and Harrah's have the best. The facilities include a wide range of fitness equipment, large pools and several hot tubs, and even food and drink service. They are not world-class, but they are the best in the city.

**Lucy the Elephant** A few miles south of Atlantic City, Lucy sticks out like a sore thumb. Visitors can have guided tours of the elephant-shaped building to learn about its history. Children are especially pleased. There isn't much to see, but the history is very interesting.

**Absecon Lighthouse** Like Lucy the Elephant, there isn't much to see or do at the lighthouse, but its historical interest alone is worth the trek to the top.

## TRAVEL SCENARIOS

Following are vacation possibilities under various circumstances. Atlantic City vacations are tremendously flexible and hassle-free. Eat when you want, explore where you want, do what you want. These scenarios keep your options open and give you the freedom to allow your vacation to unfold however you want.

## ONE-DAY GETAWAY

(**Vacation Time:** *1 Day* **Best Time to Go:** *Any time, any day*)
Atlantic City is ultra-accessible, particularly for individuals without access to a car and in a major urban area. If you fit this description, you're in luck, as your vacation can be extremely inexpensive.

Either drive or, from a major metropolitan area (such as Washington, DC, New York City, or Philadelphia), board a casino bus service to your favorite Atlantic City resort. When you arrive, spend the day roaming the resort. Check out the restaurants, the health club, the shopping, and even the beach if it is nearby and weather permitting. Stroll the Boardwalk and take in the fresh ocean air. When you're ready to return, simply board the bus (or drive) from the resort and make your way back home.

***Recommendations:*** The best resorts for strolling arbitrarily and enjoying the beach include: Tropicana, Trump Taj Mahal, and Bally's Atlantic City. Many times, however, people will want to catch a show in one of the many venues in Atlantic City. If you are interested in the entertainment, check the resort's entertainment schedules in advance, as you may not be able to buy tickets at the box office.


## ON THE CHEAP

(**Vacation Time:** *2 Days* **Best Time to Go:** *Winter weekday*)
The cheapest time to visit Atlantic City is Tuesday - Thursday in the winter, where prices for an on-Boardwalk resort can plummet to around $50 if you shop around. However, if you must stay in the summer or on the weekend, consider an off-resort hotel (you may need to rent a car if you don't already own one.)

Plan your travel so that you arrive mid-afternoon, and are able to check-in to your hotel at around 4:00 PM. Once you're situated, its time to enjoy the resort. Start off by eating an early dinner at a moderately-priced restaurant. Then enjoy the evening strolling the resort and the Boardwalk. If you're near The Walk, Atlantic City's outlet mall, you may be able to get some shopping in before the stores close. Also, since you have an entire night, you may wish to consider exploring other nearby resorts as well; so don't feel confined to the one in which you are staying. In the later hours, night owls may be able to enjoy one of several night clubs, either on-property or off. Enjoy a late-night drink before heading off to sleep.

If you're an early riser, spend the morning swimming, if your resort has a pool. Then enjoy a breakfast buffet or a quick sit-down meal. Mid-morning, check yourself out of the hotel. You are now free to explore. The Boardwalk has many shops and attractions, and a beach. But don't run around too much; this is a vacation, after all! Have a late lunch and head home in the early to late afternoon.

**Recommendations:** The best activities for a cheap vacation are those which incur little or no cover charge. Shopping without buying is free, so take all the time at The Walk, The Quarter, or other shopping venues that suit your taste. At night, Trump Taj Mahal's Casbah club is sometimes cover charge-free. If you can afford a $16 taxi ride ($8 each way), then head over to Mixx at the Borgata, which sometimes has free cover. Buffets are expensive (frequently over $20 a person); so if you can, try cheaper counter service or the various fast-food options available in each resort.

### WEEKEND WITH THE FAMILY

(**Vacation Time:** *2 Days* **Best Time to Go:** *Summertime*) **Important Note:** As stated before, family vacations can be very enjoyable in Atlantic City. However, the primary audience is adults. Therefore, children should be supervised at all times, and you must be aware that Atlantic City attracts primarily gamblers. Families with children of any age should avoid off-Boardwalk property at night. Use good judgment in all cases.

That being said, a three-day, two-night vacation with children gives you the opportunity to go beyond the Boardwalk and explore the rest of Atlantic City. You will need access to a car, because (1) access off-Boardwalk requires driving, and (2) casino bus services require passengers to be 21 or over to receive the casino discount. Additionally, there are some very specific family attractions, not-to-be-missed, which are several miles off the Boardwalk.

With a family, a summertime vacation is a must, and plan to stay at either Tropicana or Trump Taj Mahal, which are the most kid-friendly resorts in Atlantic City. While both offer coveted beach access, Tropicana has the magnificent new Quarter which features an IMAX movie theater and numerous kitschy shopping venues. Trump Taj Mahal is the closest resort to Steel Pier, Atlantic City's amusement pier.

Arrive early in the afternoon to take advantage of daylight. Almost certainly the kids will want to explore Steel Pier first, so make that a priority on day one. The late hours of the pier mean that much time can be spent here; sometimes it is open until midnight. If you need a break from the rides, Ripley's Believe It or Not! museum is nearby, and can be a pleaser for teens (younger children may find some of the exhibits scary).

For dinner, take the kids to a resort buffet (note: unfortunately, some buffets require patrons to be 21, such as the Virginia City Buffet). They are expensive but casual, and noisy kids running around may not be as much of a problem. At night, settle the kids in (if they are old enough) and have a quiet, romantic dinner or drink with your significant other.

On the morning of day two, take a swim if your resort has a pool, but don't get too tired out because Jersey Shore beach is a great place to spend the hottest afternoons. Breakfast can be had at your resort's 24-hour restaurant, but if you're still full from last night, you could get away with just that extra piece of fruit that you didn't eat from last night's buffet.

If the family is interested, Central Pier (just south of Steel Pier) is a smaller amusement pier, which features a nice go-cart track and some arcade games. There are several other major arcades on the Boardwalk that offer a wider selection of games but without the go-cart track. These attractions are best suited for older children, mostly teens.

Storybook Land is a classic South Jersey Shore destination for very young children and their families. Definitely add this to your roster and plan on at least half a day for the experience. However, for kids of any age, Lucy the Elephant in Margate is a must. A short drive south, this attraction is one of the best in the Atlantic City area. It is small and quaint and won't use up much time (the tour through the six-story pachyderm is rarely longer than 30 minutes).

If there is time, and it is hot enough, an hour or two on the Jersey Shore beach is tough to beat! Stake out a nice spot near your resort, lay down a towel, put on your sunscreen, and get comfortable. The beach by Atlantic City is generally less crowded than the surrounding Jersey Shore beaches, such as Margate or Seaside.

In the late afternoon, head back to the Boardwalk and check out Tropicana's The Quarter. The IMAX Theater here shows all kinds of movies, based on the current market. Magic Masters has all sorts of whimsical items, and The Spy Store is just plain cool. With the kids at the movies, parents can enjoy the various clubs, comedy, or dining offered at Tropicana. Spending the evening here is the best way to wrap up day two.

Sleep in on the morning of day three. You probably don't need to check out of your room until 11:00 AM, so take advantage. After a nice breakfast, head over to The Walk, Atlantic City's outlet center. In addition to the many dozens of clothing bargains, there is a range of kid-friendly stores and eating possibilities. Plus, it gives you a chance to stretch your legs before the trip home.

## BEACH AND BACKWOODS FUN

(**Vacation Time:** 2-3 Days **Best Time to Go:** Summertime) Atlantic City's close proximity to both beach and forest make it an ideal spot for people who like the outdoors, but don't want to leave the comforts of home far behind. To experience the best of outdoor activities, plan a summertime vacation.

Arrive in the early afternoon of day one. Before checking into to your hotel (you can opt for either an off-Boardwalk or on-Boardwalk resort, whichever you prefer), grab your beach towel and chair, and enjoy the hot summer sun! Jersey Shore water is surprisingly warm for a north Atlantic state.

Depending on how much you intend to do, you may decide to spend either one or two nights in the area. Relaxing on the beach is one thing, but tomorrow you will enjoy the thick wooded nature of New Jersey's largest state forest: Wharton.

On day two, load up your car and drive to nearby Wharton State Forest. Batsto Village serves as the central information area for activities in the forest, so if you're not sure what to do, head there first. Otherwise, you can hike, kayak (or canoe), horseback ride, or even camp if you have the time. The forest is large and in some places can get rather desolate.

On day three, or later in day two (depending on your schedule), jump from forested to coastal wetlands by visiting the Edwin B. Forsythe National Wildlife Refuge. Though mostly for bird-watching, the refuge provides a great long-distance view of the Atlantic City skyline, and an idea of what Absecon Island would look like undeveloped. The eight-plus-mile driving "safari" gives you some great panoramic views.

***Recommendations:*** Even though summertime offers

more activities, Batsto Village in Wharton State Forest is open year-round. There are many campgrounds, trails, and other outdoor activities throughout the forest and the rest of the Pine Barrens. The beach in Atlantic City is almost always less crowded than other places along the Jersey Shore. If you prefer more beach activity, consider going a few miles south on Absecon Island, to Margate or Longport (beach access sometimes incurs a fee in these neighboring communities, unlike Atlantic City, where access is always free). For daredevils, Lakes Bay offers some water sports. Extreme Windsurfing provides rental equipment and some training.

## ROMANTIC RETREAT

(**Vacation Time:** *3 Days* **Best Time to Go:** *Crisp, chilly winter eves, when the crowds are sparse and the luxury suites are discounted*) Atlantic City is a very popular romantic destination. Spectacular ocean views, romantic restaurants, and lavish suites of every size and description make it a couple's paradise. Though most newlyweds may prefer a more exotic destination, honeymoons and wedding anniversaries are not uncommon here.

Since romantic getaways require a romantic room, a suite in one of the resorts is a must. Suites are abundant, but be warned: on weekends and holidays, suites are frequently reserved for high-profile gamblers. Therefore, you may either need to book well in advance, or consider booking on a weekday. Jacuzzi suites are popular; they are typically a regular-sized room with a Jacuzzi and shower instead of a bathtub. The highest-priced suites, with sizes sometimes exceeding 1,000 square feet, start at around $500 per night. Oftentimes, suites might not even be available unless you are a gambler.

*Recommendations:* The nicest resort in Atlantic City is the Borgata. It is located off the Boardwalk, but if you visit in wintertime and don't expect to do much resort-hopping, this setback might not matter. Pretty much every resort in Atlantic City has at least one romantic restaurant and bar. For shopping, Historic Smithville is a peaceful place, with plenty of romantic spots, and even paddleboats on the small lake.

# WEBSITES

There are some great Internet resources on Atlantic City. When planning your trip, these websites provide additional information – in some cases, it may even be possible to purchase tickets or make reservations online. These websites are, of course, in addition to the ones that are listed with the individual attractions in this book. *Important:* this information is provided merely as a general guide; these sources are approved endorsed by the author or publisher of this book. *Use these outside sources at your own risk.*

### ATLANTIC CITY.COM
*(⌖ atlanticcity.com)* This is one of many sites that allows visitors to book Atlantic City hotel rooms online. It also has special offers and rate information for both casino resorts and non-casino hotels.

### ATLANTIC CITY CONVENTION & VISITOR'S AUTHORITY
*(⌖ atlanticcitynj.com)* This is the official website for the Atlantic City Convention & Visitor's Authority. It provides information on many of the resorts and attractions.

### CITY ATLANTIC
*(⌖ cityatlantic.com)* This website provides reviews of resorts and attractions, as well as special events and entertainment schedules.

## CITY OF ATLANTIC CITY

*(⌘  cityofatlanticcity.org)* This is the government website for Atlantic City, featuring information about the city on a more political level.

## GREATER ATLANTIC CITY TOURISM COUNCIL

*(⌘  actourism.org)* This site provides information on Atlantic City's surrounding area and regional attractions in addition to focusing on the city itself. It includes family and athletic attractions.

*Atlantic City was incorporated in 1854. The site was chosen because it was the closest accessible shore point to Philadelphia.*

# Index

# About the Author

Dirk Vanderwilt is the executive editor and creator of the *Tourist Town Guides*™ series, and author of several of the series' guides. He lives in New York City.

Books in the *Tourist Town Guides*™ series are available at book-stores and online. You can also visit our website for additional, updated book and travel information. The address is:

**http://www.touristtown.com**

## Atlantic City (3rd Edition)

Millions of people visit this vacation destination each year. But there is so much more to Atlantic City than just casinos.

Price: $14.95; ISBN: 978-0-9792043-0-2

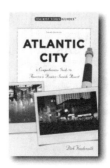

## Gatlinburg

Not just the "gateway to the Smokies" anymore, Gatlinburg is a favorite vacation destination in one of America's most beautiful regions.

Price: $14.95; ISBN: 978-0-9792043-2-6

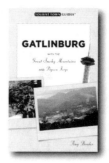

## Jackson Hole

The spirit of the American West is alive and well in Jackson Hole, and this independent guidebook will help give you the insight on the area's very best.

Price: $14.95; ISBN: 978-0-9792043-3-3

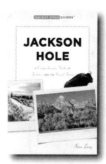

## Key West

There is much to see and do Key West. From beaches to restaurants to nightlife, this book will help plan your Conch Republic vacation.

Price: $14.95; ISBN: 978-0-9792043-4-0

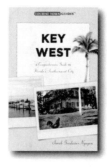

## Las Vegas (2nd Edition)

The city has become synonymous with the American ideals of vacation and pleasure. But there is much more to Las Vegas than casinos!

Price: $14.95; ISBN: 978-0-9792043-5-7

## Myrtle Beach

It is a city that has become the American answer to a tropical paradise. With this completely independent guide, get the insight on the best of Myrtle Beach.

Price: $14.95; ISBN: 978-0-9792043-6-4

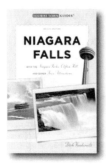

## Niagara Falls (2nd Edition)

There is so much more to Niagara than just the falls. Whether on your first or tenth visit, this guide will help you explore the many wonders that the area has to offer.

Price: $14.95; ISBN: 978-0-9792043-7-1

## Wisconsin Dells (2nd Edition)

With waterparks, wax museums, and so much to offer visitors, Wisconsin Dells is indeed a classic American vacation destination.

Price: $13.95; ISBN: 978-0-9792043-9-5

**www.touristtown.com**

## ORDER FORM #1
## ON REVERSE SIDE

*Tourist Town Guides*™ is published by:

Channel Lake, Inc.
P.O. Box 1771
New York, NY  10156

# TOURIST TOWN GUIDES™
## ORDER FORM

**Telephone:** With your credit card handy,
call toll-free 800.592.1566

**Fax:** Send this form toll-free to 866.794.5507

**E-mail:** Send the information on this form
to orders@channellake.com

**Postal mail:** Send this form with payment to Channel Lake, Inc.
P.O. Box 1771, New York, NY, 10156

*Your Information:* ( ) Do not add me to your mailing list

Name: _____

Address: _____

City: _____ State: _____ Zip: _____

Telephone: _____

E-mail: _____

*Book Title(s) / ISBN(s) / Quantity / Price*
(see previous pages or www.touristtown.com for this information)

_____

_____

_____

**Total payment\*:** $_____

*Payment Information:* (Circle One) Visa / Mastercard

Number: _____ Exp: _____

Or, make check payable to: **Channel Lake, Inc.**

*\*Add $3.00 per order for domestic shipping, regardless of the quantity ordered. International orders call or e-mail first! New York orders add 8% sales tax.*

**TOURIST TOWN GUIDES**™
www.touristtown.com

## ORDER FORM #2
## ON REVERSE SIDE

(for additional orders)

*Tourist Town Guides*™ is published by:

Channel Lake, Inc.
P.O. Box 1771
New York, NY 10156

# TOURIST TOWN GUIDES™
## ORDER FORM

**Telephone:** With your credit card handy,
call toll-free 800.592.1566

**Fax:** Send this form toll-free to 866.794.5507

**E-mail:** Send the information on this form
to orders@channellake.com

**Postal mail:** Send this form with payment to Channel Lake, Inc.
P.O. Box 1771, New York, NY, 10156

### Your Information:          ( ) Do not add me to your mailing list

Name: _____

Address: _____

City: _____ State: _____ Zip: _____

Telephone: _____

E-mail: _____

### Book Title(s) / ISBN(s) / Quantity / Price
(see previous pages or www.touristtown.com for this information)

_____

_____

_____

### Total payment*:          $_____

### Payment Information:          (Circle One)   Visa / Mastercard

Number: _____ Exp: _____

Or, make check payable to: **Channel Lake, Inc.**

*Add $3.00 per order for domestic shipping, regardless of the quantity ordered. International orders call or e-mail first! New York orders add 8% sales tax.*